The 4 Seasons of Life – by Mario Simoes ©
ISBN: 978-0-9856232-1-0

The 4 Seasons of Life

Author:
Mario Simoes

(Originally in Portuguese: "As 4 Estações da Vida")
Sao Paulo, Brazil
Published in November, 2011

Art:
Paulo Cesar Polcaro

Translated by:
Roger and Esther Schrage

Index

Recommendations

"Books that move beyond theory to life-application interest me. That's why I find The 4 Seasons of Life a compelling read. Mario Simoes moves beyond the classroom discussions of 'time management,' into the arena of how to not only define the 'season' of life you and I are experiencing, but how to live within that season a life "on purpose."

John D. Hull - *President/CEO, EQUIP Leadership (John C. Maxwell, Founder)*

"When I began reading "The 4 Seasons of Life" in English, I was inspired to read more intensely. I praise God for Mario Simoes to pen those thoughts the Lord had placed in his heart. It is totally a new concept and approach. It is not just a book; it is a workbook which challenges you to introspect and write your personal journal. Mario has written this book in a lucid style with illustrations and anecdotes. It helps you to examine your own life and assesses the season that you are in. I recommend this book as a study material in your churches, Sunday school classes and small groups."

Prof. Arthur Dhanaraj - *Vice President, International Training, Haggai Institute for Advance Leadership Training*

"It's been said, "Change is inevitable, but growth is optional." In this helpful book, The 4 Seasons of Life, my good friend, Mario Simoes, offers us timeless wisdom and insight for turning the inevitable change that new seasons bring into something positive, productive and growth-producing in our lives. Read it and grow stronger in your current season of life!"

Cal Rychener - *Sr. Pastor, Northwoods Community Church*

"Excellent for all leaders in all seasons of life. A great primer for life preparation and making a difference. Great read Mario!"

Jeff Appling *-Leadership Trainer for Equip/Senior Pastor, The Grove*

"We live in a world where most people want quick fixes to deal with their pressures, pain and problems in life. I believe that the insights that Mario has shared in this book will give needed principals and guidelines to individuals, couples and families that will change their perspective toward themselves and others. The sooner we realize that God is leading us in the different seasons of our life, we will be able to better navigate through the obstacles that we face and turn them all into opportunities. Thanks Mario for sharing your journey in the Seasons of Life."

Dwayne Betsill *- MS Psychologist, Businessman*

"Employing a familiar framework ("seasons") and easy and passionate prose, Mario Simoes invites us to consider the unique realities each of us must confront in negotiating life's rhythms and seasons. Drawing on a lifetime of rich experience and biblical truth, readers are sure to be encouraged (as I was) by a work which is straightforward and practical yet honest and deeply insightful."

Roger Taylor, *Ph.D. - President, Cuyahoga Valley Christian Academy*

"I've known Mario Simoes for twenty years and I can assure that what you are about to read will challenge your spirit. I can testify that Mario's life is a vivid example of what a true leader should be. He's not only a loving husband and father but also an investor to the new generation. Do yourself a favor and take

advantage of the wisdom in this book and apply it to your life. It will help you prepare your steps and enhance your leadership skills. And yes, there is a leader in all of us."

Adlan Cruz - *International Concert Pianist*

"The 4 Seasons of Life is wonderful! The book captures the essence of life though the eyes of one who has "been there and done that!" Recently my 15 year old son was wounded in a random shooting in a public place; an innocent bystander who's life was nearly ended by a senseless act of violence. While he survived the shooting, there is still much heartache and pain to endure.

The 4 Seasons of Life has helped me to put these events into biblical perspective. This book is filled with scriptures that will speak to your heart and give you practical ideas to help you through the Season you are in. A quick, important, and practical devotion for our times!"

David Day - *President – The Day Group*

"The 4 Seasons of Life" is a MUST read! It does not matter where we geographically live, we all experience the changing of the seasons in our own lives. This book will help you understand the "changes of the seasons" and that with God's love and hand in our lives, all things are possible. This book offers anyone the chance to learn how to love and forgive others, the same way we need to love and forgive ourselves."

Jennifer Kaiser – *Owner, The Kaiser Insurance Agency*

Acknowledgments

I want to thank my wife, and companion for life, Priscila and my two sons, Felipe and Davi for all the support, encouragement and patience they had with me while I was "giving birth" to this first book (it feels like a baby).

I thank my parents, and seasoned authors, Neco and Priscila Simoes, my in-laws, Bertoldo and Dacyr Gatz, as well as my brother Paulo Simoes, for all the encouragement to start in the "write" direction.

Thank you Roger and Esther Schrage for translating the book from the original text in Portuguese into English. Thousands will be blessed around the world because of you!

My sincere appreciation to all my friends and influential leaders around the world, who were kind enough to write a recommendation and endorsement of this book. Thanks for sharing your credibility.

I'm grateful to all the staff of the organizations I have the honor of leading, to all the members of our church I have the privilege of pastoring and to all the students I have the joy of teaching.

My deepest gratitude to Dr. David Wong for believing in me, for being the first to open the doors of international ministry and for being a friend and mentor ever since.

I thank the Haggai Institute for Advance Leadership for allowing me, for over a decade, to share my gifts in the development the leaders who are making history in their own nations all over the world.

I thank God for giving me various different seasons of life and many unique gifts and opportunities to make a difference in people's lives. I pray that this book will be one more opportunity.

I want to thank you, the reader, for choosing this book. My desire is that the following chapters will help you better understand your life and to inspire and encourage you to live it out the best way possible.

Dedication

I dedicate this book to my parents

Neco & Priscila Simoes,

whom I've had the privilege so far, of sharing with

all the Seasons of my life. They were also responsible for introducing me to the Lord of All Seasons.

Foreword

"In the morning you will take your child to the pediatrician and in the afternoon take your parents to the geriatrician, and if there is still time, you will go see your cardiologist."

In vivid and picturesque language, Mario Simoes paints for us the phases of life. Spring "is a time when you can be at peace doing nothing, simply relishing life, enjoying the moment." Summer is likened to a train engineer opening the engine full throttle, the sailor unfurling the sails to the wind, the surfer meeting the crest of the wave.

Fall "comes to our life in unexpected ways. Suddenly the winds change and the leaves begin to fall… the harbinger of the approach of a new phase in our life." I like his description of Winter best: "When the last leaf of the tree falls, Winter begins. You have reached the bottom of the well because it can't get worse. The problem ended, the bleeding stopped, and the hole in the bottom of your boat is plugged. The rain stopped and the floodwaters have stopped rising. The bill collectors stopped calling, that person has gone, the cancer has been removed, the accusations and lawsuits have come to an end. The worst of the crisis is over! The shooting has stopped, the noise has gone and suddenly you start to hear a different soft sound… the sound of silence. Winter has arrived. It is a time to repair your life."

Simoes writes as one who has seen the seasons, in his life and in the lives of people. He shares about one who calls God, "Papa Dios" (Father God) only to change it to "Papa Adios" (Father Goodbye), about "the tormentor" of his schooling days, and about time when he and his wife almost lost everything: money, dreams, friends, and sleep. He digs deep into Scriptures and spreads their words of wisdom throughout the book.

He paints powerful portraits of Jesus, Nehemiah, Moses, the children of Israel—they too lived through their seasons.

You will hear humorous tales about the lumberjacks, the hunters and the weather forecaster. You will learn why you need six friends in life and in death, what it means to "die empty" and how "opportunity it bald." Mario's style is brisk, his scope expansive, his reach, right into the heart. The reader will find himself or herself in the stories, vignettes of life, real and down-to-earth. The questions at the end of each chapter are thought provoking, and practical counsel worth whatever you pay for the book and much more.

I have known Mario for more than a decade—he wrote a song for my 50th birthday—and found in him a friend who never lets distance or absence lessen the depth of our friendship. We have served together in Maui, Hawaii, and Singapore, as well as in Brazil, and so have our wives, Priscila and Jenny.

This is his first book and I commend him for finally putting together his life's experiences and lessons. I warmly recommend it to all readers. No matter what season of life you may be in, you will find yourself in the book. More importantly, may the wise counsel of the book find a place in your life.

Rev. Dr. David Wong

Leadership Mentor - Finishing Well Ministries, Singapore

Introduction

"And God said, Let there be lights in the firmament of heaven to divide the day from the night; and let them be for signs, and for seasons, and for days and years:" (Genesis 1:14 ASV)

Life is short and time passes quickly. The memories of childhood, the vigor of youth, and the first successes as an adult seem to have happened only yesterday. There were many experiences, opportunities, joys and disappointments, hits and misses, victories and defeats, successes and failures. Each one happened at a certain time, in a period or season of your life.

Just as the four seasons of the year—Spring, Summer, Fall and Winter—rule and influence each year, there are four seasons that mark and influence each phase of our lives.

Science tells us that the planet earth makes two constant movements. The first is the rotation on its axis once every 24 hours, which determines the length of each day. The second is the revolution around the sun every 365 days, determining the length of each year.

Likewise, our life is marked by movements, cycles and seasons. Some are momentary and situational and others are part of a process that is sequential and chronological.

In the past, the Greeks used two different words to define time. The first is "kairós" which describes a time that is indefinite, situational and timeless. An opportune moment of experience and learning, considered to be the time of God. The second is "kronós", from which we get our word chronological, which measures and studies linear time, considered to be the time of men.

In this book we are looking at the four seasons of life in two aspects: the first four chapters, from the perspective of situational time, a specific moment that each season brings to our life. From the fifth chapter on, from the perspective of sequential and chronological order.

Example of the 4 seasons in a life

Job is an excellent example of someone who experienced the impact of the four seasons in his life.

"In the land of Uz there lived a man whose name was Job. This man was blameless and upright; he feared God and shunned evil. He had seven sons and three daughters, and he owned seven thousand sheep, three thousand camels, five hundred yoke of oxen and five hundred donkeys, and had a large number of servants. He was the greatest man among all the people of the East." (Job 1:1-3)

Job was the Bill Gates of his time; you can call him "Job Gates". This is what characterized the man; blameless, upright, shunned evil and he was the richest man in the East. Here we see Job in the season of Summer (subject of chapter 2). With a good tail wind, everything was going well. He was living a time of great productivity. But suddenly the winds changed and Job lost all he had.

As the story continued we read that Satan appeared before God and claimed that the only reason Job worshiped Him was that God was good to him. So Satan proposed to take away from Job all that he possessed, and God concurred but did not permit that his life be taken. Job lost his children, all his cattle, and in the end he lost all he had. Job lived the experience of Fall (subject of chapter 3), a very difficult period in his life; the phase of loss.

But the problem did not stop there. Job's situation went from bad to worse. The devil, not satisfied with this, wanted to touch him physically too and God permitted it. Then Job, who was going through a difficult Fall, confronted Winter (subject of chapter 4) and became very sick, on the edge of death.

We know of the conversations he had with his friends who hindered him more than helped. They reveal the attitude of many so-called "friends" that do the same thing today. In difficult moments they hinder more than help.

Job then passed through a severe Winter and during the whole process he continued to trust in God. He did not give up. He waited for the season to change. He expectantly awaited the coming of a new Spring. It is very beautiful to see in the last chapter of the book what Job said to God,

"I know that you can do all things;" (Job 42:2)

Would you be able to say the same thing after losing your money, children, property, health and influence? And Job adds, *"No purpose of yours can be thwarted." "My ears had heard of you but now my eyes have seen you." (vs. 5)*

How much Job learned in that Winter! He was able to understand more of God! Further along we read,

"After Job had prayed for his friends, the LORD restored his fortunes and gave him twice as much as he had before. All his brothers and sisters and everyone who had known him before came and ate with him in his house." (vs. 10)

The story is still repeated today, when things are tough for you, everybody disappears, they can't be found, but generally they come back when things get better.

"All his brothers and sisters and everyone who had known him before came and ate with him in his house. They comforted and consoled him over all the trouble the LORD had brought on him, and each one gave him a piece of silver and a gold ring. The LORD blessed the latter part of Job's life more than the former part." (vs. 11-12)

Do you remember how many animals he had in chapter one? Look at what God restored.

"He had fourteen thousand sheep, six thousand camels, a thousand yoke of oxen and a thousand donkeys. And he also had seven sons and three daughters. The first daughter he named

Jemimah, the second Keziah and the third Keren-Happuch.
Nowhere in all the land were there found women as beautiful as
Job's daughters, and their father granted them an inheritance
along with their brothers. After this, Job lived a hundred and
forty years; he saw his children and their children to the fourth
generation. And so Job died, an old man and full of years." (vs.
12-17)

Spring arrived again for Job; God renewed his life and gave him double, performing the miracle of multiplication. All the animals he had lost, God gave him double. God gave him the same number of children and blessed his life in a wonderful way. He had a new opportunity and the season of that Spring was a new beginning. Job received double what he had planted in the past, through a life that was right and just before God.

In the following chapters you will understand what season you were in when you went through certain experiences in your past. You will also discover what season you are living in right now and will be challenged to discover the opportunities, experiences and lessons God wants to teach you.

Chapter 1

SPRING

The Season of Preparing

"When a king's face brightens, it means life; his favor is like a rain cloud in Spring." (Proverbs 16:15)

Two lumberjacks participated in a competition. They each received two identical axes and headed for trees of the same size and diameter. The referee gave the signal and the competition quickly began to see who could chop his tree first. With each blow of the ax against the tree the spectators began to cheer, rooting and clapping enthusiastically.

Suddenly, one of the lumberjacks stopped and ran his finger over his ax. He then got a file out of his pocket and began to sharpen the blade. Some of the spectators were worried while the others were excited to see that their preferred lumberjack was the only one who was chopping while the other was sharpening his ax.

As the minutes passed, the lumberjack who had apparently wasted time sharpening his ax began once again to engage in the competition. He could see that his competitor was well along, having already cut through nearly half of the tree trunk.

After a series of strong and deep cuts of the ax, the two lumberjacks were tied. It became apparent that the one who had not stopped began to have difficulties. His ax struck violently against the tree; however, he could not cut deeply into the tree because his ax was dull. In contrast, the lumberjack that had sharpened his ax continued to chop his tree until it could no longer stand and it fell to the ground.

The similarity between the two lumberjacks is that both received the same tools to win the challenge set before them. However, the great difference between them was that one stopped, evaluated, planned and sharpened his ax. He won because he invested time in preparing his instrument.

Spring is the time for preparing. It is interesting to note that Spring is situated between the two most extreme seasons of the year. Spring comes right after the extreme cold of Winter and is followed by the extreme heat of Summer.

Every year, right after Winter, Spring comes. It is the time when opportunities arise, the flowers bloom and animals come out of hibernation.

It is the time to sow seeds that will one day bring forth fruit. It is the moment to prepare the soil for the next harvest. It is the moment when life blossoms.

Spring is the season to turn to studies and focus on learning. It is not the time of great accomplishments but rather the time of preparing for them. Just as the flowers renew, people also renew their goals, accept new challenges and dream of new possibilities.

Spring is the springboard to a desired future. It is a phase of freedom to dream of tomorrow. It is that special moment to evaluate, plan, prepare and chart a new course for new commitments. It is the time to plan a new itinerary for the next chapter in the book of your life, leaving that which held you back in the past and running towards the future.

The Bible speaks about the essence of this season:

"Brothers and sisters, I do not consider myself yet to have taken hold of it. But one thing I do: Forgetting what is behind and straining toward what is ahead..." (Philippians 3:13)

This is the essence of Spring. Winter is passed; now new opportunities are before us and we need to move forward. You have probably observed the cycle of the life of a butterfly. Before coming out and flying it is imprisoned in the cocoon and during this time of development it is being prepared to fly.

During our life we will pass through various Springs. Some of them will last for weeks, others may last for months and still others may last for years. For this reason we need to maximize all those times we are graced by God with the innumerable opportunities that each Spring brings to us.

One person that understood the importance of Spring for His mission and used it to the maximum was Jesus Christ. He began His ministry at thirty years of age and had a public ministry that lasted only three and a half years. Therefore, the Spring for Jesus lasted three decades. He had thirty years of preparation for three years of ministry. Notice just how important the time of Spring is in your life so that you are well prepared for the opportunities and challenges of the future.

Emotions

What emotions are manifested during Spring? Certainly this is the season which is marked by joy, confidence, love and liberty. It is a time of creativity, to dream again and a desire to learn more. It is a time to light an internal passion for life, for people and causes. It is a time to feel a new willingness to play. It is a time of positive expectations and at the same time, a moment of insecurity about the new things that are coming. If you are feeling some of these emotions, it is very likely that you are in the season of Spring.

Expected Results

What results can be expected from Spring? Certainly there is an expectation that there will be a clarification regarding your personal identity. During this period you may ask the following questions: "Why am I here?" "What am I going to do with my life?". There is an increased personal confidence as a result of a redefinition of your sense of purpose in life.

It is the time to review priorities and focus on the most important things and leave the others aside. It is a wonderful season to renew and strengthen intimate relationships with your spouse, your children and siblings. It is also a time to redefine your sense of internal value, to be more creative and improve your outlook. It is a time to dream again, to take on new risks and to launch yourself into a new life that you wish to see blossom before your eyes.

Activities

You can, and ought, to focus your attention, time and energies on the activities that contribute to making this a memorable phase of your life:

Know and research new careers

Learn of new options and opportunities in your professional arena.

Listen to old friends

There is much knowledge and wisdom among your friends and acquaintances. Ask them good questions and note the responses.

Make new friends

Take the initiative to make new friendships. Be open for new people to enter into your circle of friendships.

Return to studies

Possibly you may want to return, to college, do post graduate work, a masters or PhD, or finish that partly completed course.

Fall in love

If you are single, it is a time to fall in love. If you are married, fall in love again with your spouse! Plan a new honeymoon.

Read books

Beyond the Word of God, you need to read books that speak to your mind and heart, books that motivate you and challenge you to grow. I suggest that you set aside a Saturday to read some books and let God speak with you.

Be happy doing nothing

Spring is a time when you can be at peace doing nothing, simply relishing life, enjoying the moment and rejoicing always. How good it is to have time in which to do absolutely nothing and not feel guilty about it.

Get in motion

Get back to participating in an activity or sport, something you like to do. Engage in a sport you like: basketball, football, tennis, running, swimming or walking.

Find entertainment

Take time to listen to music, go to the theater, the movies, a museum or a concert. Learn to appreciate art and value culture.

Invest time in the people you love the most

This is the moment for you to invest your time in the people in your life you value the most: your family! Spend quality time with your spouse, your children, your parents and your siblings.

A Time to Plan

Dedicate a few days to planning a mini retreat; define and write your life mission. Define your long and short-term goals and objectives. Organize your schedule according to priorities. Prepare yourself for the Summer season that will soon follow.

Make certain that one of your greatest desires is to do the will of God and discover what He has planned for your life.

In His Word, we read: *"For it is God who works in you to will and to act in order to fulfill his good purpose." (Philippians 2:13)*

In other words, it is Him who gives us the desire to want to accomplish something according to His good will. However, due to the accelerated and fast paced rhythm of the times in which we live, we have little time to discover His purpose for our life. It is for this reason we need to take the opportunity Spring gives us to hear the voice of God and what He wants us to do in the season of Summer.

Opportunity is bald

I have taught in seminars and lectures that "opportunity is bald". It needs to be seized when it is in front of us. It doesn't do any good to run after it once it has passed because we can't catch it by the hair since there is none to grab. What is gone is gone. It was a unique opportunity to be taken. Be alert to all the opportunities that Spring brings to you.

King Solomon teaches us that *"The horse is made ready for the day of battle, but victory rests with the LORD." (Proverbs 21:31)*

We believe that God gives us victory and that we are more than conquerors in Christ Jesus, however, we are responsible to prepare the horse for the day of battle. Preparation is our responsibility. We need to do our part and God does His.

During the Spring season you will have opportunity to remove stones from your path, take away the trees that have fallen, clean the Winter mud and take away the weeds.

This is the time to free yourself from negative influences, from doubts, from pessimism, and the unbelief that some people cast over your life. Use the spade of enthusiasm to remove these destructive seeds and spread the fertilizer of faith on the good seeds, so that they grow and flourish. If you are in Spring, stop and take a deep breath and breathe the sweet smell of opportunity.

I believe so much in the importance of preparation that I have used this verb in the names of our two enterprises in Brazil: our school Preparing Generations International School and the Brand of our training firm Preparing Trainings.

Opportunity

The word opportunity historically comes from the Latin. When a ship was anchored in port waiting for high tide to sail out to sea, the sailors waited at the ready. Suddenly, when the tide was at its highest, a sailor shouted "ob portu." This was the moment when the ships untied from the pier and left the port to set sail for their destination. Ships, on the other hand, that were outside the harbor waiting to enter waited for the tide to begin to rise. Once again, at the right moment, the sailor shouted "ob portu."

Spring is the moment you have waited for. Look around you and observe the tide. If it is rising shout "ob portu." It doesn't matter if others are listening. This is your opportunity! This is your Spring.

Time to plant

God gives us many opportunities and it is necessary to take advantage of them. The fields that had been full of life, plants and fruit in past seasons are again ready to receive new seeds. They need to be planted in the Spring so that they can bear fruit in the future. Therefore, Spring is the time to plant. Don't be distracted by the beauty of the season. Don't spend it running after butterflies and forgetting to plant. Don't let yourself be molded by lazy people or permit the discouraged, unmotivated, frustrated, unbelieving and doubting people to shape your life at planting time.

Planting is work and requires discipline. There is some pain in discipline but there is also great pain in regret, in the lament of not having planted when you should have. One of my mentors, Jim Rohn, says that *"the pain of discipline weighs ounces, but the pain of regret weighs tons."*

Each year we have a harvest of fruit, vegetables and grain. Spring is a new opportunity God gives us to plant for a future harvest. Possibly today you have eaten a fruit that was planted in the Spring. This is God's nature; when we plant He sends rain in Spring so that those seeds have sufficient water to germinate, sprout and grow.

It is not sufficient to have the best seeds in the world or the best land. If God does not send rain, the seeds will die. We need Him to pour out rain on our lives, our dreams, so that they can sprout, grow and bear fruit.

God says: *"I will send rain on your land in its season, both autumn and Spring rains, so that you may gather in your grain, new wine and olive oil." (Deuteronomy 11:14)* God is saying; "Do your part, plant. I will send the rain at the right time and you will see the results."

You will reap what you sow. If you plant pineapples you will harvest pineapples.   If you plant corn seed, you will harvest corn. If you plant seeds of love, of joy and of forgiveness, these are the fruits you will harvest.

Spring in your profession

Perhaps you are in a Spring season in your career. High school and college are excellent examples of Spring because you are choosing an area of study or preparing to enter the labor market that represents Summer. Or perhaps your Spring is returning to study for a masters or doctorate.

Another example of Spring in your profession is transition in the work place, a change of career, company or specialization. The most difficult phase in this transition is unemployment, which characterizes Fall.

Life is like a game of soccer; it is divided into two periods of forty years, with a half-time between. This half-time happens generally when you reach your forties. As much as possible, take advantage of the half-time by participating in a retreat or seminar that will help enable you evaluate your strong points, your mission and your passion. In this way you will sharpen your ax so you can be certain that when your second half comes it will be more strategic, fruitful and productive.

Spring in your marriage and relationships

All relationships, especially marriage, go through various cycles of seasons. Sadly, some die or are destroyed during severe falls and winters. The secret for maintaining a healthy marriage is to use the Spring seasons to strengthen and plant, with good seeds, the fertile soil of the heart.

Just as engagement was preparation for marriage it is necessary to capitalize on Spring to live a new honeymoon, date, travel, dine out and take walks together. Take time to exercise, converse, read, pray, love, dream again, make plans and renew the commitment as a couple.

Spring guarantees a good result for the couple during Summer and prepares them for the unexpected arrival of Fall or Winter.

The danger of Spring

The great danger of Spring is to ignore its importance and try to move quickly to the great accomplishments of Summer.

History is filled with examples of individuals, companies and nations that failed because they did not pay particular attention to preparing.

You probably have seen army scenes where the sergeant gives the order to his soldiers; "ready, aim, fire."

There is an order to be followed by the soldiers to assure that they hit their chosen target. However, many follow the orders of "another sergeant" that orders; "fire, aim." They say: "Prepare? Don't bother? Why? What for? It's not necessary?" They fire first and afterwards look for the target.

According to specialists in time management, every hour invested in preparation saves ten hours of work.

"Ready, aim" is part of Spring. "Fire" is part of Summer.

Therefore, do not hurry this stage, don't rush or pass over this season, because if it is omitted you will end up "burned out."

Preparing the soil

It is interesting to observe that the soil only will return that which is planted. It does not transform an orange seed into a strawberry. Whatever you plant, the soil returns. All that you plant in the Spring you will reap in the future, depending on the showers of blessing that God pours out on your life. The soil will return only that which is planted.

The apostle Paul begins verse 7 of Galatians 6 with this phrase: *"Do not be deceived."* Why does He say this? Simply because many times we deceive ourselves on this subject. He continues by saying; *"God cannot be mocked. A man reaps what he sows."*

Sometimes we plant the wrong seed and hope to reap good fruit. Let us paraphrase this text; "Folks, don't deceive yourselves or mock God who created all this process of planting. To do this is to mock Him. After planting a bad or wrong seed, you expect to reap good fruit. Worse still is when you plant nothing and want God to perform a miracle and cause good fruit to appear where nothing was planted. That is not how God functions."

The truth is that we need to plant. God established processes and laws and if we respect and obey them, we will reap all that we plant.

What sort of harvest do you want from your life, your family and your career? Fill your hands with these seeds and plant them in Spring. Do you want to reap love? Begin to plant love in your home. Begin to plant respect and you will reap respect. You will reap in the future that which you plant today.

The soil returns to you multiples of what you have planted. This is the miracle of multiplication. In the parable of the sower Jesus declares that some seed fell on good soil and gave a harvest of thirty, sixty and one hundred for each seed. What a marvelous miracle! God could say; "Since you planted one seed you will only reap one fruit". But this is not what He does.

When you plant one seed He turns it into a fruitful tree that will produce much fruit. Each fruit will contain more seeds that will produce more fruitful trees, and so it goes. This is the cycle of multiplication.

The God of Spring

God wants to bless us with much more. In the parable of the sower Jesus explains that which is sown in good soil is like the one who hears and understands the Word of God. Then it will produce a harvest of one hundred, sixty and thirty fold. When we sow and obey, we can expect a multiplied harvest in our life. When we obey God's principles to love, respect, serve our neighbor and invest in the Kingdom of God, most certainly we will reap fruit in abundance. However, for this to happen we need to hear and obey the Word of God.

Talking with one of my students enrolled in the International School I asked: "Do you have control of your opportunities?" He told me, "No." I then asked him another question; "Do you have control of your preparation?" He answered; "Yes, I do." Then I continued: "If you prepare yourself and suddenly an opportunity appears, what will happen?" He answered: "I'll be successful."

We can control our preparation because God allows us this control. We need to prepare and sow so that God can send us opportunity. When opportunity encounters our preparedness, it produces success and the miracle will take place.

Perhaps you are going through Spring. Take advantage of the opportunities that God is giving.

You prepare, plant good seeds, plan, dream of great things and wait to receive many blessing from God.

Questions for reflection

1. Have you had some Spring seasons in your past? Describe them.

2. Are you in a Spring season today? What are the characteristics of Spring in your life now?

3. What are the things you can do now to take advantage of the opportunity of Spring?

4. What are the lessons that God wants to teach you during Spring?

5. Is someone close to you passing through Spring? How can you help him/her?

Chapter 2

Summer

The Season of Producing

"Go to the ant, you sluggard; consider its ways and be wise! It has no commander, no overseer or ruler, yet it stores its provisions in Summer and gathers its food at harvest". (Proverbs 6:6-8)

There were years of preparation, waking at dawn to train, long hours of running, followed by grueling muscle exercises, stretching and weight lifting. Great discipline was necessary to maintain a restricted but nutritious diet. Many other activities were laid aside and omitted to focus solely on that competition, in that country, in that city, in that stadium, at that hour. Everything was ready. Eight athletes were on the track, bent down with their hands on the starting line. The stadium, filled with euphoric spectators, went silent. One could only hear the sound of clicking cameras and the rapid heartbeat of each heart. In those seconds it seems that the earth stood still. All was ready, waiting that much anticipated moment... the sound of the firing of the starting gun.

For the train engineer, Summer is the time to open the engine full throttle; for the sailor it is time to unfurl the sail to the wind; for the surfer it is the crest of the wave; for the driver it is time to put the "the pedal to the metal"; for the runner it is the time to fly low.

Everyone knows that Brazilians drive fast and fly through traffic. One day a Portuguese tourist came to Brazil having heard that the taxi drivers fly low. With great anxiety he got into a taxi in Sao Paulo. The driver asked him where he wanted to go and he responded "I want to go up Brigadeiro Luiz Antonio Ave." The driver asked, "How high up do you want to go?" To which the Portuguese tourist responded brusquely, "If you go higher than five feet I'll kill you."

Summer for the hippy is good vibes, but for the Christian it is being in the blessing. All joking aside, Summer is the hottest season of the year; it is the time of much activity, high productivity and great accomplishments.

Even as there are various changes in climate, temperature and vegetation in Summer there are various changes in our life when we pass through this powerful season.

Emotions

As we go through this season we all feel great self-confidence and courage to face new risks and challenges. It is a time of great energy and joy in the accomplishments. It is the time to be fulfilling the purpose for your life. It is a phase of many challenges and of feeling fulfilled for producing, overcoming and winning. At the same time, a person, by being occupied with an excess of work and many activities, ends up neglecting his health and letting go of closest friends.

On the other hand, many are stressed during this time due to tiredness. Others feel isolated since they are moving at such a rate that few can follow them. However, generally the people who go through Summer are passionate about what they are doing and for the people around them.

Expected Results

The first aim is to carry out the plans and goals made in Spring. It is a time to seek the best of life, exerting yourself to reach the top, be it in your profession, your relationships or your academic life. Summer is certainly a time to crave success in all you do. It is the time to make things happen, to grow in your career, to be creative, to make money, buy, assume new risks, make changes, increase your family, produce and feel fulfilled.

Activities

Expand your network

Summer is the time to expand your network of friends and strengthen the bonds of friendship with the people you have journeyed with for some time. Be intentional with your commitments.

Travel

Get to know new places, new pathways and have new experiences.

Manage your time

During Summer your time is in short supply, therefore you need to know how to use it well. If you don't, the press of day-to-day life will prevent you from doing what you should.

Seek balance

You need balance between your professional and family life, between your public and personal life. Remember that you gain nothing by conquering the world and losing your family along the way.

Invest in quality time

Because of the lack of available time, you need to give quality time to your family, your spouse, your children, your parents and siblings. Learn to be present where you are. Turn off the TV and cell phone and dedicate all your attention to the person you are with.

Develop hobbies

In the midst of so much work it is important to develop a physical activity or hobby where you can relax, unwind and refresh. You can lift weights, walk, ride a bike or swim. Dedicate yourself to something that helps you disconnect from your professional intensity. Allow this activity to renew your energy, reinvigorate your soul and contribute to your general well being.

Care for your soul

A man went on a safari to Africa. He was delayed because of connection problems and arrived after the expedition had left.

He couldn't accept that fact and hired some porters and a guide and started out in search of the expedition. They advanced rapidly under the scalding sun but still did not catch up with the expedition. They rested and early the following morning before sunup hurried out, but still did not catch the group. On the third day the man wakened everyone early and they frenetically rushed the entire day without rest but still were unsuccessful. On the fourth day, once again he went to waken his guide and porters but no one moved; "Get up. Let's go. Today we'll catch them!" The guide responded; "My good Sir. We have run three days without stopping and we are exhausted. We are not leaving here until our souls catch up with us."

The ant

God uses nature to speak to us and teach us. Have you seen ants carrying a leaf or twig that weighs four or five times itself?

"Ants are creatures of little strength, yet they store up their food in the Summer." (Proverbs 30:25)

It is incredible how the ants know the exact time to cut the leaves and twigs and carry them tens of meters to their nest. The ant stores them there because he knows that soon the season will change and Fall and Winter will come.

"He who gathers crops in Summer is a prudent son, but he who sleeps during harvest is a disgraceful son." (Proverbs 10:5)

The fruit

Therefore, it is wise to harvest that which was prepared and planted in Spring. What is it that God wants of us in the Summer season? He wants us to bear fruit.

His will for our lives is that we bear fruit. He did not create us to simply live, grow, pay the bills and die. He created us for a marvelous purpose! When we act upon what we have received from Him: our gifts and talents, our knowledge, creativity, resources, our influence and our health, we begin to bear fruit. God created us for this.

"So God created mankind in his own image, in the image of God he created them; male and female he created them. God blessed them…" (Genesis 1:27-28a)

Notice that the first thing God did after creating man and woman was to bless them. What a wonderful thing it is to know that we have God's blessing in our lives. After He gave a blessing he gave an order.

"Be fruitful and multiply, and fill the earth, and subdue it; and rule over the fish of the sea and over the birds of the sky and over every living thing that moves on the earth." (Genesis 1:28b NASB)

With this order God gave other responsibilities as well.

"Then the LORD God took the man and put him into the Garden of Eden to cultivate it and keep it." (Genesis 2:15 NASB)

God gave him the order to multiply, be fruitful, cultivate and care for everything He placed in his hands. This is our responsibility; God expects us to live fruitful lives.

If you were called to render an account of your life, how much fruit would you have to offer to God? How would you carry it? Would it be by the train load? By a truck load? A basket full? A bucket or a plate full? What is your current harvest of fruit?

As we saw in the last chapter, *"It is God who works in you to will and to act in order to fulfill his good purpose." (Philippians 2:13)* That is, God wants you to be a blessing since it is for this reason He blessed you. It is for this He placed in you the desire to know the will of God. Who knows, you may discover God's will through a frustrating experience that will provoke in you a "holy discontent." (To borrow a term from my friend Bill Hybels, pastor of Willow Creek Church, in Chicago). This discontent may lead you to discover a response to a problem and a solution to that frustration.

My wife Priscila and I went through this some years ago in relation to the schooling of our sons, Felipe and Davi. We became very frustrated with what they were learning in school. What they learned at home was promptly unlearned in school. The values and principles that we taught at home were contradicted and despised in the classroom. So we decided to be part of the solution, not part of the problem. We resolved to start a school that would make a difference in the lives of the students- not only to inform, but also to form their lives so that they can transform the world.

Believing in the vision and dream that *"To change a nation, we must change a generation"* we founded in Brazil the Escola Internacional Preparando Gerações (Preparing Generations International School) in 2001.

A phrase that has most impacted my life was written by a man I know and profoundly admire, Dr. John Haggai, founder of the Haggai Institute of Advanced Leadership.

"Attempt something so great for God that is doomed to failure if God isn't in it."

This is what God did. He placed in our hearts His desire, and suddenly we began to dream of something we wanted to accomplish for God. Who knows how to work to reach and influence children, young people, couples, families, professionals and entrepreneurs? These dreams become desires that burn in us and will continue to burn until they are accomplished.

How can you know if a desire is really God's will or simply a momentary personal wish? The difference can be seen over time. Your personal wishes come and go, by contrast, over the years though the will of God may diminish, but it never leaves your heart.

God has a desire, a call, and a purpose for your life. When you say to God; "Here am I, Lord," He listens attentively.   Then you begin to work, produce and feel an incomparable sense of fulfillment.

We need God to discover and pursue His desire for us; however, beyond this, we need Him to help and equip us to accomplish His good will. Therefore, the will of God is not only good, but perfect and full of joy.

"Yet he has not left himself without testimony: He has shown kindness by giving you rain from heaven and crops in their seasons; he provides you with plenty of food and fills your hearts with joy." (Acts 14:17)

A successful life

There are various definitions of success, and mine is very simple; ***"Success is to discover and fulfill God's purpose for my life."***

In the day you stand before God, He will have two questions. The first is "What did you do with my Son, Jesus Christ? Did you accept or reject Him as your Savior and Lord?"

The Bible is clear and says that whoever has the Son of God has eternal life, but he who does not have the Son of God, does not have eternal life. Therefore, if you say that you accepted Jesus as your only Savior and Lord, He will say; "Wonderful. Very good! Enter and live with me forever."

The second question is: "What did you do with the life I gave you?" It will not help if you say that you built many houses, had many cars, occupied many important positions at work, received numerous degrees and titles, and became famous and influential. None of these will help you if you did not know and fulfill the call and purpose of God in your life.

I hope that you respond to the second question in the following way: "God, you gave me the ability to teach, for this reason I taught many students around the world. You gave me the ability to be an entrepreneur, to start some companies, to create many jobs and to influence many people. I was faithful and just and used what you gave me to expand Your Kingdom."

If you are a mother, fulfill your purpose and be the best mother in the world and invest your life in the life of your children. If you are a grandmother, be a special grandmother. You were chosen by God to be fruitful.

In the end, if you are a veterinarian, doctor, musician, soldier, athlete, professional, businessperson, entrepreneur, clerk or pastor, it is not important what your profession is. You need to know and fulfill God's will and purpose for your life. Most certainly you will be a great success in this world.

You were chosen

Who does not remember back in grade school when teams were being chosen in physical education class? The teacher picked two players who alternated in choosing the rest of their respective teams. When there were eleven students in the class, only five could play on each side. The captain went along choosing. Seven remained, and then five, then three and finally one remained who was left out.

Did this ever happen to you? You were left out by your friends? It's a terrible feeling to not be chosen, isn't it?

In my own life I have gone through various experiences of not being chosen.

But isn't it great to be chosen, to know that someone called you out to be part of the team. You will not be spending your time on the bench watching the others play.

Know that a marvelous God is the true "captain of life" and when He chose His team He chose you. He pointed at you and said "I want you for my team, you will not sit on the bench watching. I choose you."

God chose you not because of the number on your jersey, but He called you personally by name. Jesus said: *"I chose you and appointed you so that you might go and bear fruit—fruit that will last." (John 15:16)*

God wants you to bear much fruit. Not fruit that comes once in a while, but good fruit that remains. Praise God, we were chosen; however, with this choosing comes a great responsibility-we must bear fruit.

The question is, "Where will I bear fruit?" You are to bear fruit where you are, wherever you are planted. You were planted in your home, therefore bear fruit there. You were planted in your school, in your university, in your company, in our society and world. If God planted you in these places, it was for you to bear fruit that remains.

One day your children will leave home, what will happen in their life then? If you planted in them you can relax knowing that they will be bearing fruit wherever they go.

God planted you in the place where you work. Possibly within a few years you will not be working there any longer. So while you are there, bear fruit. In the future people will remember the difference you made in that place and in their lives.

Die empty

Summer is the most favorable season for you to achieve and accomplish your best. It is one of the best, if not the best. Therefore, if you are studying, learn all you can; if you are in the labor market, produce, earn, multiply, create, protect, invest, love, influence and give all you can. Do all this and when you arrive at the end of your life, you will be empty of yourself and full of satisfaction.

Andrew Carnegie, one of richest men in the world in the last century, accumulated a fortune which at that time was worth billions. Someone once asked him, "Now that you have made all this money, what are you going to do with it?" He replied, ***"I have spent my whole life earning this money. From now on it is my purpose to give it away. In the second half of my life I will see to it that this money gets into the hands of those who need it most."*** That is how he became one of the greatest philanthropists of the last century. He invested in schools, universities, libraries, hospitals and scientific discoveries for the good of mankind.

Certainly this man died empty, because he took nothing with him. Our greatest example of a giving life is not Wesley, Carnegie or Haggai but rather the man with the greatest influence in human history: Jesus Christ.

"Very truly I tell you, unless a kernel of wheat falls to the ground and dies, it remains only a single seed. But if it dies, it produces many seeds." (John 12:24)

Jesus not only taught this principle, but He lived it, dying on a cross to give us life. Therefore, we also need to die in order to give what we have received. We need to give the best of our knowledge, the best of our resources and the best of our influence. How do we do this? What did Jesus say in regard to this?

"I am the vine; you are the branches. If you remain in me and I in you, you will bear much fruit; apart from me you can do nothing." (John 15:5)

If you wish your life to bear much fruit, the secret is to remain in Jesus Christ and Him in you, 24/7. When you leave for work, invite Him to go with you as a passenger to watch you drive and behave in traffic. If you are a student, invite Him to go with you to your classes. If you are an entrepreneur, invite Him to be with you in your office. If you are a "domestic engineer", permit Him to participate in your activities. Ask Jesus what He would do in the moment of crisis or threat. He is always present in your life, in the midst of problems, struggles and difficulties.

Without Jesus we can do nothing! Without Jesus you may have a lot of activity but little productivity. What you accomplish is like burning straw, it is smoke that will soon be gone and nothing will remain. However, with Jesus you can do anything. The Bible tells us *"I can do all this through him who gives me strength." (Philippians 4:13)*

The danger of Summer

For all the good of Summer, there is also a great danger. It is called working too much and those who are affected by this malady turn into workaholics. These people are addicted to one thing-- work, work and more work!

This has been one of the greatest dangers in modern society, causing premature heart attacks in men and women of 40 or 50 years who are stressed out by overwork. Work is good; in excess it is dangerous. Apparent professional and financial success is not true or sustainable when it is reached without God's presence, His values and principles.

"Papa Dios"

Many years ago when Priscila and I lived in Puerto Rico we knew a businessman named Luiz. He was active, full of energy, very connected and apparently very successful. Every time we spoke with him of Jesus, Luiz said that he didn't need God since he was so successful. Then he would show us his wallet stuffed full of dollars saying that money was his god because it took care of him and gave him what he needed.

However, God has a way of getting the attention of people. After a bit, Luiz got sick and landed in the hospital facing the life threatening surgery. At that time my dad visited him in the hospital and spoke to him one more time of Jesus, His love and God's plan for his life. Worried about his future, Luiz finally asked Jesus to be his Savior. Through many tears he promised God that if He would cure him and save his life, he would serve Him for the rest of his life when he got out of the hospital. I remember that moment as if it were today.

All of us were moved by the decision that he had made. Everything went well, both in the surgery and in the post op. During the days of recovery he read the Bible, "God's word" all the time. He prayed "Papa Dios" ("Father God" in Spanish) here and "Papa Dios" there. But when he was released from the hospital he returned to his activities, stopped praying, stopped reading the Bible and stopped going to church and disappeared. Sadly he forgot "Papa Dios" and traded it for "Papa Adios." ("good-by Father" in Spanish)

The example of this man is very common these days. Perhaps you know someone who is living this way or it may even be you who is living this way. Be careful. Don't forget God in your Summer season.

This problem is not peculiar to today. The church in the past also experienced this. In the book of Revelation God says:

*"I know your deeds, your hard work and your perseverance. I know that you cannot tolerate wicked people, that you have tested those who claim to be apostles but are not, and have found them false. You have persevered and have endured hardships for my name, and have not grown weary. Yet I hold this against you: You have forsaken the love you had at first."
(Revelation 2:2-4)*

Never abandon your first love for God, no matter how bad your situation.

Summer in your profession

In Spring you were seeking a change of life, work, business or career, but perhaps in Summer you have begun this new endeavor. This is the phase in which to take risks, to face the unknown, to confront great challenges and take advantage of new opportunities. Continue investing in your life; in your personal development. Remember, *"Everyone gives what they have."* You need to be energized and enthusiastic to go forward and encourage those beside you who depend on your motivation and determination to succeed.

Invest in and add value to people in creative ways through your attitude, words and actions. People are the greatest resource you have. Stay focused on your goals but stay ready to adapt in the face of the unexpected. As a surfer, adjust to the wave of productivity because it can take you to places you have never been before.

Summer in your marriage and relationships

Summer, for a couple, is a time of maturing. It is a time for working together or in separate careers, but for the same purpose. It is a time to build something together- save, buy a house and enlarge your family. It is a time when children come and expand life, challenges and joys to your family. Take care that the day-to-day routine, the tiredness from all the commitments do not suffocate and destroy the love between the couple. To prevent this from happening seek to pray together. Go out for a romantic dinner; take a weekend off at a hotel for romance, conversation, dining and resting. It is worth it!

Find out what your children like to do. Invest quality time individually with each child. He/she will never forget this.

The leader in Summer

I want to conclude this chapter describing the life of a great leader and man of God who had a very fruitful Summer. His name is Nehemiah.

Having been born in captivity, Nehemiah had experienced the Fall and Winter seasons. One of the worst moments of his life was when he heard of the condition of his beloved Jerusalem, the city of his fathers. After weeping and suffering for his people, Nehemiah entered a new season, Spring. Over four months, after receiving the bad news, he began to develop a plan for the repair and reconstruction of the walls of Jerusalem. Nehemiah presented it to his boss, Artaxerxes. He received approval and the resources to go ahead with his plan for the reconstruction of the walls of Jerusalem. He traveled with a military escort carrying materials and much money for the work.

Upon arrival in Jerusalem he made a hidden survey of the walls of the city. Afterwards he met with the city leaders and told them his plans. Still in his Spring, Nehemiah explains: *"I set out during the night with a few others. I had not told anyone what my God had put in my heart to do for Jerusalem. There were no mounts with me except the one I was riding on. Then I* said to them, 'You see the trouble we are in: Jerusalem lies in ruins, and its gates have been burned with fire. Come, let us rebuild the wall of Jerusalem, and we will no longer be in disgrace.' I also told them about the gracious hand of my God on me and what the king had said to me. They replied, 'Let us start rebuilding.' So they began this good work." (Nehemiah 2:12, 17-18)*

God placed His desire in the heart of Nehemiah (vs. 12). The second chapter of the book of Nehemiah describes in detail the Spring season in which there are dreams, plans, energy and a disposition to take risks. Then beginning in the third chapter we see Spring come to an end and Summer begin and continue to the end of the book. *"Eliashib the high priest and his fellow priests went to work and rebuilt the Sheep Gate." (Nehemiah 3:1)*

It is clear that beginning at this point they moved into the accomplishment of that project. Everyone began to work side by side; everyone doing his part to reconstruct the walls of the city.

The energy and productivity of Summer were so great that they exceeded their original goals. *"So we rebuilt the wall till all of it reached half its height, for the people worked with all their heart." (Nehemiah 4:6)*

They had a tail wind; working, watching, carrying, producing, building, painting, decorating, praying, singing, accomplishing in a few days that which had been destroyed and abandoned for more than seventy years.

It is common in Summer to have obstacles appear. They spring up and attempt to impede the work and progress. This is what happened with Nehemiah. Some people tried to distract him by telling him something like this, "You are working too much. You need to rest some. Stop a little. Let's take a coffee break." Nehemiah's response was; *"so I sent messengers to them with this reply: 'I am carrying on a great project and cannot go down. Why should the work stop while I leave it and go down to you?'" (Nehemiah 6:3)*

What an example of a leader. He was at the peak of his mission, focused on the results, experiencing incredible productivity and he did not want to be distracted by anything. There was one end result of this determination; mission totally accomplished.

"So the wall was completed on the twenty-fifth of Elul, in fifty-two days. When all our enemies heard about this, all the surrounding nations were afraid and lost their self-confidence, because they realized that this work had been done with the help of our God." (Nehemiah 6:15-16)

The will of God was accomplished through the life of Nehemiah. He began his career well and ended it even better. He understood how to overcome the dangers of Summer and confront his enemies without forgetting his God during the whole process.

For this same reason God has also called you to a life full of action, productivity and overflowing with victories that could never be accomplished without the help and blessing of God.

The God of Summer

The greatest part of the ministry of Jesus Christ was accomplished during the season of Summer. He produced, bore fruit, healed, cast out demons, rebuked, taught, loved, forgave, influenced, made disciples and gave Himself for all humanity.

There were thirty years of preparing-- Spring. However, in the city of Cana of Galilee, in the middle of a wedding feast, the starting gun was fired!

The water was turned to wine, launching the greatest three and a half years of Summer ever recorded. This Summer changed the history of the world to the point that we divide time before and after His life. (BC and AD)

Take advantage of your Summer. Work, produce, accomplish, harvest, protect, love, make a difference and fulfill the purpose for which God created you!

Questions for reflection

1. Have you already gone through Summer seasons? Describe them.

2. Are your presently in Summer? What characteristics of Summer are present in your life?

3. What actions should you take to take advantage of your Summer?

4. What are the lessons God is trying to teach you in Summer?

5. Is someone near you experiencing Summer? How can you be of help to that person?

Chapter 3

FALL

The Season of Stopping

"Light is sweet, and it pleases the eyes to see the sun. However
many years anyone may live, let them enjoy them all. But let them
remember the days of darkness, for there will be many.
Everything to come is meaningless." (Ecclesiastes 11:7-8)

A group of hunters were dropped off in the woods by a single engine plane. It was to come back in seven days to take them home with the animals they had hunted. After a week of very successful hunting, they came back to their campground and found the plane waiting. Upon placing the animals in the baggage compartment the pilot said, "I think all the animals you shot are too heavy for the plane to get airborne!" The leader of the group responded, "Don't worry. Last year we hunted the same amount and it fit in without any problem." The pilot consented and everyone got in the plane and took off. Right after a difficult takeoff the plane suddenly started to lose altitude and it fell into some trees. Miraculously, no one was hurt. One of the hunters asked the leader of the group, "Do you have any idea where we are?" To which he responded, "I think we are about a half mile from where we fell last year."

The interesting thing this story shows us is that we need to learn to carry less baggage; how to deal with loss, how to listen to other people and above all, how to learn from our mistakes.

Fall starts when the first leaves float gently to the ground, thus beginning the season of loss, struggles and tests. Fall has no favorites; it touches everyone, even those who have done nothing to deserve such difficulties.

The first leaf to fall from the tree may come as a fight in your marriage or a text message on your cell phone. The fall may come by an e-mail telling you that you have lost 50% of your investments or may come in a meeting where your employment is terminated. The first leaf may also fall with a phone call informing you of the death of a loved one. It may also fall with a report from your medical exam or of someone else in your family.

It is very probable that you are remembering right now a time when fall once came to your life. It was a time of loss--perhaps your spouse, children, health, job, business deal, finances, and with this you wound up losing control of your life. All this caused you to lose peace, sleep, your dreams, your vitality, and perhaps even your will to live.

"Even the stork in the heavens knows her appointed times; and the turtledove, the swift, and the swallow observe the time of their coming. But My people do not know the judgment of the Lord." (Jeremiah 8:7 NKJV)

Desert

Often Fall is compared to a desert. You probably heard the expression, "I'm going through a desert." The desert is an arid, hostile and uninhabited environment. During the day it is scalding hot and at night the cold is harsh. A person is very vulnerable. The desert is a place without water and food, where people rarely survive. Fall certainly is the season most hostile and difficult of all.

It is interesting to note that fall also comes to our life in unexpected ways. Suddenly the winds change and the leaves begin to fall. It is the harbinger of the approach of a new phase in our life. It is possible that a person can experience this season in any stage of life. This truth is confirmed in the Word of God, *"But let them remember the days of darkness, for there will be many." (Ecclesiastes 11:8)*

Fall, therefore, is a season which we will go through many times throughout our lifetime. Jesus confirmed this saying, *"In this world you will have trouble." (John 16:33a)* In other words Jesus is saying, "In your life you will go through several falls." The question is, "How are we going to face it? In whom are we going to place our confidence when we are going through them?" Jesus concludes by saying, *"But take heart! I have overcome the world." (John 16:33b)* That is, "If I have overcome the world (fall), I will also teach you to overcome fall in your life."

Thanks be to God that we have Jesus Christ as Savior and Lord of our life. Through Him, God loves, teaches, helps, encourages, orients, guides, blesses and protects us. Not because of a religion but because of a personal relationship we have with His Son.

I want to highlight that in the majority of cases, fall is not the result of sin. Many Christians have a tendency to spiritualize things and think the fact that someone is going through difficulties and trials is because they are in sin. No. This is far from the truth! Yes, there are times the justice of God places a heavy hand on those who choose to disobey Him. For these people, life is not Fall or Winter, but rather hell on earth. And if they do not repent while there is still time, they will live eternally in the true hell. Therefore, do not judge anyone for the problems they are going through.

Emotions

Fall is the season of very strong emotions. The first sensation you have is one of decline, totally contrary to what you experienced in Summer. That was a time of growth and excitement. You lived a hectic life, running from one place to another, but now the picture is very different.

In this season you feel imprisoned by pressure with no place to go. Fall generates a strong sense of things being out of whack and you can't believe what is happening. The pain is intense, the suffering is great, the sadness is profound and many times the anger toward those who caused your hurt is uncontrollable. The fact of being betrayed, especially by those you have helped so much, leaves your heart bitter. As a result of all this you may experience depression.

In Fall it is common to have some people disappear from your life. It is also common as a leader to have a sense of defeat. You feel like a failure and frustrated by being unable to find a solution to the problems you face. Your self-esteem has fallen through the floor.

Expected Results

The greatest desire we have in Fall is to get out of this season as quickly as possible. We want it to end soon because we want to get right back to Summer so we can work, love, produce and continue our normal life with its great achievements.

Another outcome we seek is to settle accounts. Not only our financial accounts, but our accounts with other people. We want to see justice, preferably by our own hand, wanting people to pay for injustices they have done. Life is unfair! The truth is that only one person has the right and power to bring justice to this world--God, the Just Judge.

I believe, however, that the most important result we can hope for from Fall is simply to survive. Our focus is not to plan, create, and produce but rather to endure the struggles and survive this season in the hope that the next one will come as soon as possible.

Activities

In this phase it is important to create a contingency plan to help face the intense winds of Fall.

Consider other alternatives

If the loss was a relationship or health, emotional, financial or professional issues, look for possible alternatives which were not present before the problem arose.

Spend more time with fewer friends.

Many friends who were "best friends" disappear from your life in Fall. However, thankfully a few friends remain! "Blessed is the man who comes to the end of his life with some good friends beside him." (1 Mario 1:20)

An excellent place to find friends is in church. There, for the most part, you will find sincere people who accept and love you unconditionally. It makes no difference if you have money or not, if you are having difficulties or not, these people are willing to walk with you whatever the cost. One of life's worst experiences is to go through struggles and difficulties alone. This is the reason God created the church, the family of God, so that together we could love Him and our neighbor as ourselves. It is essential to have friends and brothers and sisters we can count on no matter the time of day or night.

Seek the right help

One of the biggest errors many commit is to ask counsel of the wrong people. There are many well intentioned people who give terrible advice. Do not seek counsel from just anyone about marriage, family, business, finances or relationships. Seek help from someone who is capable.

Seek help quickly

Fall is the time to seek the help of God and of qualified people. Look for a counselor, a pastor, a coach or a specialist in the area of your difficulties. Do not make the same big mistake that many do of "just let it be and see how it turns out."

Many let the problem fester to the point that it becomes almost irreparable. If you see indicators of potential difficulties, promptly seek the help of capable people. This is the secret of Formula 1 racing. They have found that the more quickly the medical car arrives at the site of an accident, the better the chance of the driver surviving.

Seek the right person at the right time.

Get a check-up

Take the opportunity to go to the doctor and take a battery of tests to determine your physical condition. When all is said and done, your best years are still to come and you need a healthy body to go forward.

Exercise

The time has come for you to exercise, even if you don't want to. It is important to be physically active. Participate in a sport you enjoy; run, walk, swim, but don't just sit there doing nothing.

Travel

Get away from where you are. Spend a day or weekend with a friend or in a hotel or B&B. This is a healthy thing to do. Simply breathing new air in a different place may reinvigorate you in your Fall.

Watch inspiring films

Go to the movies or rent an inspiring DVD of adventure and achievement. These will certainly touch your heart or even make you cry. (Some examples are: Chariots of Fire, Facing the Giants, Mr. Holland's Opus and The Sound of Music.) You will be inspired by people who passed through difficult Falls, even worse than yours. The day will come when you will thank God for sustaining you in the midst of such difficulties.

Read books

Beyond daily Bible reading, develop the habit of reading good books. Read motivational books, leadership books, biographies, self-help books that will renew your mind and heart to move forward and not give up.

Find hope

Perhaps you are not responsible for the events that brought you into this Fall; however, you are responsible to do what you can to maintain your spirit with faith and hope. The prophet Jeremiah teaches us a thousand year secret,

"Yet this I call to mind and therefore I have hope…" (Lamentations 3:21)

Light at the end of the tunnel

The good news is that *your Fall will end some day*. Life will not be an eternal Fall. If you are in the middle of this season, the good news is that it will not last forever. The only thing that will last forever is God's love for you.

Most of the time Fall comes quickly and leaves veeerrryy slooooo wly. It doesn't help to fight it. It would be like going out dressed in shorts and T-shirt, wearing sun glasses and sandals carrying a beach umbrella and calling, "Hey everybody, let's go to the beach."

Some Falls may last days, weeks, months or, I'm sorry to say, years. However, just as certain as the seasons change; your Fall will pass.*"There is a light at the end of the tunnel, but this time it's not the train."*

Peace amid difficulties

Peace is what we most need to confront and overcome the difficulties of Fall. The world out there may be in flames, there may be a thousand problems and difficulties, but if you have peace you will be able to face any problem. But what sort of peace? The world offers several cheap and false versions of peace. They may have immediate effect but few lasting results; liquor, drugs and pleasure offer momentary relief. You may even forget your problems, but when the effect wears off, the pseudo peace is gone as well.

The hard reality is that the problems return, increased by the hangover, headache, vomiting, guilt, a heavy conscience, doubt, fear, sadness and unhappiness.

There is another peace however, the true peace that lasts and can only be found in Jesus Christ, who is the "Prince of Peace." He said, *"Peace I leave with you; my peace I give unto you: not as the world giveth, give I unto you." (John 14:27)* and He adds, *"These things have I spoken unto you, that in me ye may have peace." (John 16:33)*

"What", not "Why"

God uses the circumstances of life to teach us new things. The question we most ask in Fall is; "Why did this happen? Why did God do this to me?" We always want to know the why of everything. We want to know who is responsible, who to blame. However, you need to ask another kind of question; "What does God want to teach me in this?" If you ask this question your eyes and ears will be open to hear God's answer.

I want to share a short section from the book "Being God's Man… In Tough Times" by Stephen Arterburn, Kenny Luck and Todd Wendorff that tells the story of a man who went through a long Fall.

"Ten years ago I convinced my wife Denise, to move to a distant city for an excellent job. Not long after having moved far from our family and friends I lost that job. It was a terrible experience. This was not what I had wanted to happen. I was confused. I then had the idea to open my own business and we went five months without any income. Denise and I were nearly out of money. To make matters even worse she got sick and we struggled to find answers. Then I became depressed. I was frustrated with God, wondering why He allowed all this to happen to me. I wanted the situation to change quickly and get out of the depression. I wanted a better life, but it didn't come. I remember asking God to be present with me in those days, but He was silent. Like Job, I sought a solution to my problem in the Throne room. Then one night, I felt the need to read the Bible."

I want to quickly pause here before continuing the story. You already have seen that he went through one of those stormy Falls! How often God uses these Falls to speak to us. In Spring He tried to speak to us but we were too busy admiring the butterflies and flowers that we forgot the Author of creation. How many times during the busyness of Summer-- working, making money and producing we forget God? Suddenly He says, "I know how to talk to you. Now you will listen!" This is the only way that God could get us to say; "OK, I will stop." It is the blessed stopping of Fall. Now let's go to the rest of the story.

"I opened to Proverbs 3:5-6, 'Trust in the LORD with all your heart and lean not on your own understanding; in all your ways submit to him, and he will make your paths straight.' God was speaking to me and I could feel His presence. It was as if a light that had gone out had come on again. Denise and I looked at those years as the worst, but they turned out to be the best of our lives! Denise was healed and I got a new job. After

this our family became much more united. Our faith grew, we found new friends that helped us in our difficulties."

Perhaps this is your story. Don't ask God why. Ask what you will learn and what He will teach you during your Fall.

We all go through difficulties. However, the important thing to know is how you react in the midst of adversity. This makes all the difference.

If you have a positive attitude, and are open for God to teach you, most certainly this season will be shorter. But if you complain and keep asking why, why, why, it is possible that the season may last longer than necessary. The faster you learn, the shorter your Fall.

First "proving" then "approving"

We are speaking of "proving" which means to go through tests or trials. For example, to enter college you need to take a college entrance test to be approved for the course. In life, however, many are not "approved" because they did not pass the tests of that season. God allows people to go through trials to prove their character and know if they really learned to deal with their relationships, work, business, health or family.

This brings to memory a time when I was in high school in Sao Paulo. Our Portuguese teacher was known as the "school tormenter." In each class she would chose some students for an oral "quick quiz." "Mario Simoes, let's see what you know." I still shiver when I hear those words. During that quiz the teacher came down hard on the student that had not studied or done his/her homework. However, those that did well were praised highly.

You are only "approved" after being "proven." Do you know what the desire of God's heart is? That you be approved. Just as any teacher who gives a test wants his students to be approved.

"Do your best to present yourself to God as one approved, a worker who does not need to be ashamed and who correctly handles the word of truth." (2 Timothy 2:15)

Therefore, read, declare and live the Word of God so that you do not need to be ashamed to present yourself to God.

Every time you go through a time of proving it is a sign that you are finishing a phase in your life. By passing the test you will be ready to start a new deeper and more intimate phase, a new season in your relationship with God.

Jesus himself went through Fall when He was denied, betrayed, beaten, falsely accused, and unjustly crucified. He suffered the loss of His family, His friends, His disciples and then even his life. However, He was approved.

"Jesus of Nazareth, a man approved of God" (Acts 2:22 ASV)

"Son though he was, he learned obedience from what he suffered and, once made perfect, he became the source of eternal salvation for all who obey him" (Hebrews 5:8-9).

Test of faith

We can rest in the fact that God will test those He loves. *Hebrews 11:17* speaks of the heroes of faith, *"By faith Abraham, when God tested him, offered Isaac as a sacrifice."* God proved Abraham. He is considered the father of the Jews, the father of our faith, the man from whom our inheritance has descended. If God tested Abraham, He will also test His children. God allows us to go through Falls to test our faith. Years ago God tested the children of Israel;

"Observe the commands of the LORD your God, walking in obedience to him and revering him. For the LORD your God is

bringing you into a good land—a land with brooks, streams, and deep springs gushing out into the valleys and hills; a land with wheat and barley, vines and fig trees, pomegranates, olive oil and honey; a land where bread will not be scarce and you will lack nothing; a land where the rocks are iron and you can dig copper out of the hills.

When you have eaten and are satisfied, praise the LORD your God for the good land he has given you. Be careful that you do not forget the LORD your God, failing to observe his commands, his laws and his decrees that I am giving you this day. Otherwise, when you eat and are satisfied, when you build fine houses and settle down, and when your herds and flocks grow large and your silver and gold increase and all you have is multiplied, then your heart will become proud and you will forget the LORD your God, who brought you out of Egypt, out of the land of slavery. He led you through the vast and dreadful wilderness, that thirsty and waterless land, with its venomous snakes and scorpions. He brought you water out of hard rock.

He gave you manna to eat in the wilderness, something your ancestors had never known, to humble and test you so that in the end it might go well with you. You may say to yourself, "My power and the strength of my hands have produced this wealth for me." But remember the LORD your God, for it is he who gives you the ability to produce wealth, and so confirms his covenant, which he swore to your ancestors, as it is today."
(Deuteronomy 8:6-18)

What a beautiful text. God tested and proved His people in the past, proved their faith to see what was in their hearts. It is not by your strength neither by your knowledge. Be careful not to think that you are so powerful or that everything depends on you. Or to think that it was the strength of your hand and your knowledge and intelligence by which you have achieved. God can make all that disappear from one moment to the next, and yet He does this so that you can know to trust in Him.

How is your faith? What is the size of your God? Is he a god of Sunday, a god of the weekend, a god of religion or is He the true God always with us?

Some may even say that they are very much shaped by the difficulties of life. It is in the difficulties that God molds our character and life.

"Consider it pure joy, my brothers and sisters, whenever you face trials of many kinds, because you know that the testing of your faith produces perseverance. Let perseverance finish its work so that you may be mature and complete, not lacking anything." (James 1:2-4)

It is God speaking to us through the life of James, who simply wrote these words. In reality this process has the objective of molding, polishing and preparing us. Since we have God in our life, we need nothing else.

My personal Fall

I have gone through various Fall seasons in my life, however a few years back I passed through the most difficult of all. My wife, Priscila, and I experienced the loss of friends, substantial financial loss, loss of dreams and also the loss of sleep. Many times we prayed and cried out under so many pressures and struggles, not knowing what to do. We had no idea how we would get out of that situation. They were very difficult days, the likes of which I would not wish on anyone. However, we knew that God was always with us. He was faithful, as He always is. Sometimes the answer came as the clock was striking midnight, but it always came. Sometimes we opened the refrigerator and there was almost nothing, but God was faithful.

One of the phrases my mother always said to me in that Fall was this, ***"Not everything bad is bad. God knows everything."***

How true this is. In some sort of way we began to see what God wanted to teach us and bit by bit we learned many lessons. I believe that this was one of the greatest learning times in our lives. The other day Priscila said to me, "Sweetheart, thankfully we never gave up. We are now harvesting fruit in the lives of our students."

While we are in the depths of Fall we recognize our incapacity and impotence to accomplish anything. At the same time we recognize that God has the power to take us out of that situation, lift us up and strengthen us.

What for us is a time of loss is a time of gain for God. He uses strong winds to blow away our excess baggage, unnecessary tools, unhealthy relationships, bad habits, and confidence in our own ability. He does a "spring cleaning" in our lives to prepare us for a future He knows and plans for us.

It is very probable that soon you will be helping other people who are going through what you are going through today. Therefore, learn your lesson well so you can teach it well to others. Remember: ***"Your sufferings today may become your teachings tomorrow!"***

"Praise be to the God and Father of our Lord Jesus Christ, the Father of compassion and the God of all comfort, who comforts us in all our troubles, so that we can comfort those in any trouble with the comfort we ourselves receive from God." (2 Corinthians 1:3-4)

This book is proof of this. If I had not experienced the challenges and lessons of each season in my own life, I certainly would not have been able to write these chapters. Today I understand and thank God for all my experiences, both good and bad.

The great lifeguard

A group of people went to a park with a beautiful lake. Many went swimming since the day was warm and sunny. After a time, some saw a young man in the middle of the lake begin to shout, flail and go under. Happily for everyone, there was a national swimming champion in the group. Everyone looked at the swimmer expecting him to quickly jump in the water to save the young man. But he deliberately took off his sneakers and shirt and waited, watching the youth flail around. That bothered some of the spectators who shouted; "Hurry up, go get him."

But the lifeguard just waited and waited while the youth in the water was thrashing around weakly, just trying to survive. When the young man was just about spent, the lifeguard dove into the lake, reaching him with just a few strokes. He grabbed the young man and brought him to the shore, saving his life.

Some people went over to the lifeguard to ask why he had delayed since it was only a matter of seconds before the young man would have drowned. He responded that he had waited for just the right moment because if he had reached the young man while he still had a lot of strength, he might have grabbed him around the neck and drowned them both. He explained that he first waited for the young man to expend all his strength. Once he saw that the young man was totally spent, he knew it was the right moment to save him.

How many times is God at the lakeshore of our lives, ready to save us while we continue flailing about, using all our energy and knowledge trying to survive?

We ignore the fact that we cannot save ourselves without the help of a "lifeguard". In fact, Jesus is the great and only "lifeguard" of humanity. But He is waiting for a gesture on your part, a word saying, "God, I need your help. Only you can save me! Save me!" Then He responds, "Now I will take you out of the lake of difficulties and you will know that I am the Savior of your life."

God not only wants to be your Savior, but also to be your Lord, to guide and direct your life. God's purpose was never to be a 911 number, simply to be called upon when you need help. God does not want to be an "SOS God" that is, called upon only when you have an emergency and then after He saves you to forget Him and go on your way. What God wants is that you have a daily, constant and eternal relationship with Him.

God wishes to manifest His power in our lives not only to save us, but also to be with us at all times, in all situations and in all seasons.

"But we have this treasure in jars of clay to show that this all-surpassing power is from God and not from us. We are hard pressed on every side, but not crushed; perplexed, but not in despair; persecuted, but not abandoned; struck down, but not destroyed. We always carry around in our body the death of Jesus, so that the life of Jesus may also be revealed in our body." (2 Corinthians 4:7-10)

Fall in your profession

If you are unemployed, consider the following alternatives, "Should I stay in the same field? Change my career? Think of starting my own business? Go back to school to strengthen my resume?"

Invest in yourself by reading good books, taking courses and continue your personal development so that when this season ends, you will be prepared.

Talk with good friends and choose someone to be your counselor or coach for this phase of your life.

Open your heart to God and ask Him to show you the way that

you should go. Take advantage of this "half-time" of the game to review the best and worst moment of the first half. Seek to learn from them and make the tactical and technical adjustments for the second half.

Remember that your profession should be linked with your passion, gifts and talents. Who knows, perhaps it is the time for you to stop working to fulfill the dreams of others and to start pursuing the dreams God has for your life. ***Only you can transform these dreams into reality.***

Fall in your marriage and relationships

Generally, when a man goes through difficult times he retreats into his "cave". He doesn't talk or converse with anyone, but his mind starts working, looking for alternatives or escape routes from his problems. Consequently, he may pass many nights without sleep. On the other hand, in most cases when a woman has a problem, she goes to the top of the mountain, and there in a loud voice for all to hear she proclaims all she is feeling and experiencing. The "mountain" may be the beauty shop, the club, the women's group at church, her friends, Facebook, e-mails or any woman willing to listen.

During Fall, many couples experience conflict due to extreme financial pressures. Unemployment, debts, and problems at work often bring couples to opt for separation. But this is not the best solution. There is hope. I can assure you that your Fall will come to an end.

Simplify your lifestyle. Cut out nonessential expenses but do not cut or diminish your love for each other. With God's help you will pull through. Together you will overcome and emerge victorious.

A people in Fall

The people of Israel were slaves in Egypt for about 400 years. God raised up Moses as their leader to take them to the Promised Land. After experiencing the great miracle of crossing the Red Sea on dry land, the people had a great celebration.

"Then Moses led Israel from the Red Sea and they went into the Desert of Shur. For three days they traveled in the desert without finding water. When they came to Marah, they could not drink its water because it was bitter. (That is why the place is called Marah.) So the people grumbled against Moses, saying, 'What are we to drink?' Then Moses cried out to the LORD, and the LORD showed him a piece of wood. He threw it into the water, and the water became fit to drink.

There the LORD issued a ruling and instruction for them and put them to the test. He said, "If you listen carefully to the LORD your God and do what is right in his eyes, if you pay attention to his commands and keep all his decrees, I will not bring on you any of the diseases I brought on the Egyptians, for I am the LORD, who heals you." Then they came to Elim, where there were twelve springs and seventy palm trees, and they camped there near the water."   *(Exodus 15:22-27)*

Moses and the people had gone three days without water to drink when they arrived at a place where the water was bitter. Then the people started to complain to their leader, "Now, why this? We were doing so well in Egypt. There we had good water to drink and here we only have bitter water." Moses was directed by God to take a piece of wood, a bush and throw it in the water. This wood is a symbol of Jesus Christ, who was crucified on a cross. When we let Jesus take care of our problems, He is able to transform our bitter water into sweet water to quench our thirst. Sometimes we may be surrounded by water, but is still not sufficient to satiate our needs. When we call on Jesus to take care of our problems in Fall, He performs a miraculous transformation in our life.

The people drank the transformed water and then went on to an even better place, Elim, where there were twelve springs and seventy palm trees. There they could drink all they wanted. The truth is that Elim, the destination God had for the people, is the place of much water. In the meantime, He took His people to an obligatory stop at Marah to test them and teach them.

In your Fall, God possibly has taken you to the obligatory stop at a place like Marah to see how you would react to the test. Remember that Marah is not your final destination and you will not stay there always. However it is there that God wants to do a miracle in your life and then He will take you to a much better place--a place where His plans and purposes for your life will be accomplished.

The God of Fall

Perhaps you are angry with God for the things that were lost in this Fall season. While you maintain this attitude you will be distant from God and the great love He has for you.

When I was a kid I often disobeyed my parents and as a consequence, I was corrected. But right after that unpleasant experience I received a hug and a kiss and heard these words, "I love you, my son!" They knew that for me to learn to obey my parents and later to obey God, the time of correction was necessary. Nevertheless it was difficult for me. Then before leaving the room I always said these words; "I love you too. Thank you for correcting me."

Fall is a time of correction, love, forgiveness, and learning to obey God. During this time we need to understand that He wishes to teach us and prepare us for the next season of life.

Therefore, God is the Lord of Fall. He wants to use this season to be the Lord of your life, of your family, of your company, your studies, your business dealings, your children, your career and all you have. There is nothing better in this world than to turn your life over to God and allow Him to be the Lord of all that we are and have.

Questions for reflection

1.   Have you already gone through Fall seasons? Describe them.

2.   Are your presently in Fall? What characteristics of Fall are present in your life?

3.   What actions should you take to take advantage of your Fall?

4.   What are the lessons God is trying to teach you in Fall?

5.   Is someone near you experiencing Fall? How can you be of help to that person?

Chapter 4

WINTER
The Season of Repairing

"It was you who set all the boundaries of the earth; you made both Summer and Winter." (Psalm 74:17)

A film crew was shooting in the Rocky Mountains. An Indian came to the director and said; "Tomorrow it's going to snow!" But the director ignored him. The following day, in the middle of the shooting, clouds covered the sun and it began to snow and ruined the scenes for the day.

One beautiful day, a few days later the Indian came back again and said; "Tomorrow it's going to rain!" But again he was ignored. The following day during the shoot the winds changed and a cloudburst ruined the scene.

The director called his assistant and told him; "Find that Indian and hire him to work for us. We are not going to shoot another day without first checking with him." The Indian was hired and he accurately forecast the weather of the area.

One day the Indian did not come to work and the director sent his assistant to get him. When the Indian arrived he told the director; "I'm sorry, but I can't help you anymore." "Why?" asked the director. "Do you want more money?" "No" said the Indian, "my radio broke."

Many times when a solution is found it seems so simple and obvious. You do not need an Indian to tell you that the season is changing.

Winter is one of the most extreme seasons of the year. The low temperatures force people to go inside the house or other warm places. Many animals withdraw and pass the season in hibernation. Most plants have bare branches, having lost all their leaves. Likewise, the Winter season of life is a time when we close down and withdraw. We also hibernate for a period of withdrawal, reflection and recovery from the intense winds of Fall.

Due to the extreme activity and weariness of Summer and the losses and wounds of Fall, Winter is a time to rest and care for your body. Beyond this, it is a time to care for your soul and renew your downcast spirit.

Winter begins with the ending of the struggles and difficulties of Fall. When the last leaf of the tree Falls, Winter begins. You have reached the bottom of the well because it can't get worse. The problem ended, the bleeding stopped, and the hole in the bottom of your boat is plugged. The rain stopped and the floodwaters have stopped rising. The bill collectors stopped calling, that person has gone, the cancer has been removed, the accusations and lawsuits have come to an end. The worst of the crisis is over! The shooting has stopped, the noise has gone and suddenly you start to hear a different soft sound... the sound of silence. Winter has arrived. It is a time to repair your life.

Emotions

The feelings of anger toward the people who hurt you in Fall still exists in this phase. The sense of loss, sadness and often fear of the unknown still persist. For many it is a time of solitude and isolation. An example of this is that when you are invited to a party, you prefer to stay home. This is normal. You prefer to be alone and not have people come by; you are closed in your cocoon.

On the other hand, there is the freedom from the struggles and a relief that the tension has ended, but you still need treatment. In this phase you prefer to be quiet. You don't want to talk a lot and feel best reflecting and meditating.

Expected Results

"Rest at last." What you want most in Winter is to rest and sleep. Winter is a phase in which you need spiritual renewal and personal growth. What you really want is inner peace. This is the time to strengthen the friendships with those few who remain from Fall. They are your true friends. This is a time to review your life and reflect on what has happened in the past and start to look to the future. Seek to develop a new sense of purpose. Start to ask, "Why am I here? What are the lessons God is trying to teach me? How do I need to change?" In Winter you need to renew your confidence that was shaken in Fall.

Activities

When Spring comes again you will plan a new start in your life. However, until that time there are some activities that will help you in your Winter phase.

Take a spiritual retreat

Go away for a weekend, or if possible a whole week, and dedicate some days to seeking God. Many times it is necessary to get away to be able to hear the voice of God. It is known as the Sabbath time. The Bible says, *"Be still, and know that I am God." (Psalms 46:10)*

Get counseling

Seek counsel from people who won't judge you for being in Winter and who understand what you are going through and can help and guide you in this important phase of life.

Dedicate time to your friends

Be intentional with the people that are at your side. Learn the following from my friend Giba, who is 6 foot 7 inches tall; "A true friend is the one who has to kick the gate open when he comes to your house." You may ask "Why". "Because his hands are full of steaks for the barbeque."

Do you know how many true friends you need at the end of

your life? The correct answerer is "six". You are going to ask "why?" Because you will need one friend for each handle on your coffin.

Keep a journal

Understanding that your tendency will be to isolate yourself in Winter, do something that fills your tank. Set aside time for music, art, sports, exercise and activities that relax you while at the same time keep you in motion.

Spend devotional time with God

Without doubt, Winter is a good time to read the Bible and spend more time talking with God. It is a time to fill yourself with the Word of God and bring your soul to Him.

Read books and watch films

As in other seasons, take advantage of this time to read motivating books and see inspiring films that can be used by God to encourage your heart.

Care for your body

Often the crisis of Fall causes anxiety that triggers many people to eat in excess. Consequently this may cause an increase in weight. Find a nutritionist and watch what you eat. At the same time try to walk and exercise regularly. In the beginning your body may complain but the benefits are worth it.

Relax

It is important to regularly get a relaxing therapeutic massage. Find a good professional and you will feel the difference in our body. Another recommendation is to go to a sauna, at least once a week. It will help eliminate toxins from your body and will improve your immune system.

Take an inventory

Take this time to do an inventory of your life, your errors, your successes, your talents, your passion, your calling, your family, marriage, ministry and service to others. Use this opportunity to see where you can improve.

Time of evaluation

It was the great Greek philosopher Socrates who declared, *"The unexamined life is not worth living."*

Once you finally have the courage, ask your spouse to evaluate you. "Honey, how can I improve as your husband/wife?" Be ready to hear what you don't want to hear. In my house, God speaks to me through a feminine voice, the voice of my wife.

If you survive this experience, also ask your children how you are doing as a father or mother. I can guarantee that they will tell you the naked and cruel truth.

Winter is also a time to correct our errors. I can assure you that it is much easier to learn from other people's mistakes. Beyond this, Fall is notorious for showing us our failures and Winter is a good time to correct our mistakes.

In the last Winter of our own lives, right after that financial Fall, I saw that it was easier to blame someone else than recognize my own part in the process. I assumed responsibility for my part and started to correct my errors. It was not the easiest thing in the world, but it was important to do this.

God uses the chill and separation of Winter to teach us something new. When you are going through Winter you ask, "Where did I go wrong? What do I need to change or improve?" If you are asking these questions, I guarantee that Winter will be shorter than you imagine.

God wants to use you to make a difference in the world, but to do this; He needs to make a difference in you. God uses all the seasons of the year to do this, but especially Winter.

Only people that have been changed and transformed can be used by God to change and transform the world.

This is the work of God, the covenant He has with you to change your world first. In Fall God wants to test your faith, in Winter he wants to mold your character.

You don't need to change to become someone else. You need to change to be the person God wants you to be. If you weren't you, who would be you in your place?

"He changes times and seasons; he deposes kings and raises up others. He gives wisdom to the wise and knowledge to the discerning." (Daniel 2:21)

Time of healing

"Weeping may stay for the night, but rejoicing comes in the morning." (Psalms 30:5)

Several years ago I went through a Fall in the area of ministry and relationships. There were months of conflicts, accusations, criticisms and gossip that ended with a split in the ministry and dissolution of various relationships. Just the same the conflict continued in an indirect way for some time. The image that came to my mind was from old movies of cowboys and Indians. The Indians attacked the cowboys and to protect themselves they circled the covered wagons in order to defend and protect themselves as best they could. The Indians, on the other hand, circled the wagon train, shouting and shooting their arrows.

My family and I felt like we were the cowboys at the time. We were attacked from so many sides, by so many arrows that flew over our heads and we had no place to go. Unfortunately, that season lasted several years, until the time that I could stick my head out of the wagon and say, "Wow, there are no more arrows."

How good it was to feel that sense of relief. That was the moment that my Winter began. I started to experience a time of healing. The arrows had ended, the crisis had passed and I needed healing for my physical, emotional and spiritual wounds.

The psalmist says, *"He heals the brokenhearted and binds up their wounds." (Psalms 147:3)*

Only God can cure, heal and tend to our wounds. Oh how Fall leaves its wounds! Just as the trees lose all their leaves in Fall, leaving the branches exposed, God removes our masks and coverings to show us who we really are. It is an uncomfortable feeling, but necessary to identify our errors and begin a period of healing and repair.

The same thing happens when you go to the doctor with a cough. The first thing he does is to get an X-ray to see how your lungs are. Just like the leafless tree. God also has an X-ray of our inside to see the reason for our pain.

Many people think that others are to blame for their pain, but God is a specialist in curing people and He wants to cure your life during Winter. You only need to let Him do it.

Winter may last weeks, months, and even years. This will depend on two factors: the gravity of the damage and loss you had in Fall and also your disposition to permit God to act in your life in your Winter.

We want Winter to end as soon as possible because we are anxious to enter Spring and then quickly on to Summer. But it will not help for you to try to hurry it along; Winter will last as long as necessary. The absence of a crisis does not mean you can return to the normalcy of the past. Outside everything can be tranquil, but inside areas still exist that need to be healed and renewed in your life. It is necessary to be very prudent in your Winter.

A leader in Winter

Moses lived his first 40 years in Egypt. In spite of being an Israelite, by a miracle of God he was adopted by the daughter of Pharaoh. As such he learned all the knowledge of the Egyptians; he had servants, status, title, money, fame and power. In other words, an eternal Spring. Who said that it was eternal? God had another plan and calendar for Moses. By killing the Egyptian soldier, Moses entered a deep Fall, in which he lost all that he had and fled to the desert of Midian.

Without servants, palaces, chariots, comfort and ease, he now became a shepherd; beginning a Winter that would last 40 years.

After this season, now 80 years of age, Moses begins his Summer, liberating and leading the people of Israel to the promised land for another 40 years. Moses' Winter only ended when he surrendered to the call of God on his life. If he had not obeyed God it is very probable that his life would have ended there. His best years never would have happened, and certainly the Bible would have a different story--imagine Joshua and the Ten Commandments.

The poison that cures

There are people who, because they have been hurt, decide to never trust anyone again. They close themselves off for fear of being "bitten" again.

Nature, however, teaches us an effective principle. The antidote that can cure someone is extracted from the same snake poison that can kill them.

How often when we are injured by other people we have the tendency to want to disappear; "If only I could get away from all this down here and go live on top of Sugar Loaf Mountain!"

If this could happen, Sugar Loaf Mountain would soon be overflowing and the problem would be even bigger. The words of others often deeply wound us but it is also through other people that God brings the cure for us.

"The words of the reckless pierce like swords, but the tongue of the wise brings healing." (Proverbs 12:18)

How can you know if you are cured? The answer is simple. When you can forgive the person who injured you. When we repeat the Lord's Prayer we declare, *"Our Father in heaven, hallowed be your name, your kingdom come, your will be done, on earth as it is in heaven. Give us today our daily bread. And forgive us our debts, as we also have forgiven our debtors." (Matthew 6:9-12)*

This text explains that God will forgive us in the same measure that we forgive the people that injure us. If you do not forgive, God does not forgive you.

Forgiving someone is one of the most difficult things in the world to do. When we are not able to forgive someone, we carry that person with us all the time. Imagine yourself carrying someone on your back all day; when you go to work, there he is weighing down your shoulders; when you go to sleep he is on your mind. This is why many have nightmares, because they have the person in their mind all the time. This scene may seem strange, but the truth of not forgiving is a burden and it is only lifted when you forgive. God wants to show His love to others through your forgiveness.

"Be kind and compassionate to one another, forgiving each other, just as in Christ God forgave you." (Ephesians 4:32)

Love is completely connected to forgiveness and forgiveness to love. The life of Jesus' disciple Peter shows that the question of forgiveness is not a new one, that it is just as difficult today as it was in the past.

One day Jesus was talking with His disciples when this theme came up.

"Then Peter came to Jesus and asked, 'Lord, how many times shall I forgive my brother or sister who sins against me? Up to seven times?' Jesus answered, 'I tell you, not seven times, but seventy-seven times.

Therefore, the kingdom of heaven is like a king who wanted to settle accounts with his servants. As he began the settlement, a man who owed him ten thousand bags of gold was brought to him. Since he was not able to pay, the master ordered that he and his wife and his children and all that he had be sold to repay the debt.

At this the servant fell on his knees before him. 'Be patient with me,' he begged, 'and I will pay back everything.' The servant's master took pity on him, canceled the debt and let him go.

But when that servant went out, he found one of his fellow servants who owed him a hundred silver coins. He grabbed him and began to choke him. 'Pay back what you owe me!' he demanded.

His fellow servant fell to his knees and begged him, 'Be patient with me, and I will pay it back.'

But he refused. Instead, he went off and had the man thrown into prison until he could pay the debt. When the other servants saw what had happened, they were outraged and went and told their master everything that had happened.

Then the master called the servant in. 'You wicked servant,' he said, 'I canceled all that debt of yours because you begged me to. Shouldn't you have had mercy on your fellow servant just as I had on you?' In anger his master handed him over to the jailers to be tortured, until he should pay back all he owed.

This is how my heavenly Father will treat each of you unless you forgive your brother or sister from your heart.'" (Matthew 18:21-39)

Have you forgiven that person who caused you so much pain? Have you extended forgiveness to those who betrayed and harmed you?

Pray now, forgiving these people. Say, "God, I forgive _____, in Jesus' name. Amen." Forgive and you will be forgiven.

Ready for Spring

How will you know that Winter has ended, that you are cured, ready to turn the page and begin the preparation of Spring? The answer is simple, when the pain is gone.

If you have a scar in some part of your body, remember how this process began. Probably it was a result of an accident or surgery. Once they had finished stitching you up, the place remained very painful. After a few days as the scar was forming, you still felt the pain. Then after time passed you made a great discovery, when you touched the scar, the pain had disappeared.

This tells you that Winter is over! The scar will always be there, but the pain will never return. The scar is a reminder of the crisis or difficulty of the Fall you went through.

Winter in your profession

Take the opportunity of Winter for reflection to evaluate your work and career.

I remember deciding to leave an organization after passing

through a particularly arduous Fall in my professional ministry. That very same day I went to a retreat led by my friend Bud McCord. That weekend I was able to learn to abide in Jesus!

Some months later I attended a "Life Plan" retreat led by another friend Tommy Nelson, in which I was able to write my personal mission statement and develop my life plan. I am still reaping the fruit of those retreats that I participated in during my Winter. They made a difference in my life.

Winter in your marriage and relationships

Use this time to spend more time together. Take an inventory of your marriage, celebrate what is going well and correct that which needs improvement. It is important that you talk about dissension that you have had and forgive each other. The future of your marriage depends on this moment when forgiveness is extended.

God casts our sins into the depth of the sea and then places a big "No Fishing" sign on the buoy. Seek God and rest in this truth.

Be an instrument in the hands of God to bring healing to your spouse. Think of creative ways to show your love. Don't forget to always say "I love you."

These same principles should be used with your children and the other people with whom you have relationships.

The God of Winter

Winter is the season to be ready to make changes in your life, your character and your behavior. Winter is the time when God wants to work on you. In the book of Jeremiah God is compared to the potter and man to clay in the hands of the potter.

"This is the word that came to Jeremiah from the LORD: 'Go down to the potter's house, and there I will give you my message.' So I went down to the potter's house, and I saw him working at the wheel. But the pot he was shaping from the clay was marred in his hands; so the potter formed it into another pot, shaping it as seemed best to him.

Then the word of the LORD came to me. He said, 'Can I not do with you, Israel, as this potter does?' declares the LORD. 'Like clay in the hand of the potter, so are you in my hand, Israel.'" (Jeremiah 18:1-6)

I don't know if you have ever watched a potter at work. He uses a wheel on which he places the clay. He spins the wheel with his feet and then, little by little, with his hands on the clay he shapes the clay, for example, into a vase. But suddenly, if the vase bends and Falls, the potter takes all that clay again, and begins the shaping process all over.

Winter is like that. You are the clay; all of us come from the dust of the earth. God is the potter and He begins to mold us into a new vase. We often sing; "Mold me and make me, after thy will." It is much easier to sing than to allow God to place His hand on our life and begin the process of molding us after His will.

In this process He runs into a pebble that needs to be taken out, and this hurts. But God knows that this small pebble, a small flaw in our behavior, will destroy the vase when it goes in the oven to be fired.

For this reason during Winter, God takes you by the hand, and with great care removes impurities, shaping the clay to make your life a work of art.

"For I am the LORD your God who takes hold of your right hand and says to you, Do not fear; I will help you." (Isaiah 41:13)

Extra, extra, extra!

Here is great news! *"See! The Winter is past; the rains are over and gone." (Song of Solomon 2:11)*

What a change of life! Winter, the time of reflection, correction, forgiveness and healing; that seemed to last an eternity, has finally gone. Turn the page, open the window, see the sunlight, feel the breeze on your face and breathe deeply!

It is time to put on new clothes, gather your family and friends and have a party. You are ready to begin a new life!

Questions for reflection

1.   Have you already gone through Winter seasons?

2.   Are your presently in Winter? What characteristics of Winter are present in your life?

3.   What actions should you take to take advantage of your Winter?

4.   What are the lessons God is trying to teach you in Winter?

5.   Is someone near you experiencing Winter? How can you be of help to that person?

The 4 Seasons of Life

In chronological order

"There is a time for everything, and a season for every activity under the heavens." (Ecclesiastes 3:1)

There was a man that had four sons. He wanted his sons to learn, not to judge things too quickly. So he sent them each on a quest, in turn, to go and look at a pear tree that was a great distance away.

The first son went in the winter, the second in the spring, the third in the summer and the youngest in the fall. When they all had gone and returned, he called them together to describe what they had seen.

The first son said the tree was ugly, bent and twisted. The second son said it was covered with green buds and full of promise. The third son disagreed; it was laden with blossoms that smelled so sweet and looked so beautiful, it was the most graceful thing he had ever seen. The last son disagreed with all of them; he said it was ripe and drooping with fruit, full of life and fulfillment.

The man then explained to his sons that they were all right, because they had each seen only one season of the tree's life. He told them you cannot Judge a tree, or a person, by only one season.

That the essence of who they are, and the pleasure, joy and love that come from that life can only be measured at the end, when all the seasons are up. If you give up when it's winter, you will miss the promise of your spring, the beauty of your summer and the fulfillment of your fall. Don't let the pain of one season destroy the joy of the rest. Don't judge life by one difficult season.

Persevere through the difficult patches and better times are sure to come in time. Aspire to inspire...before you expire. Live simply. Love generously. Care deeply. Speak kindly and leave the rest to God.

Happiness keeps you sweet, trials keep you strong, failures keep you humble, success keeps you growing, but only God keeps you going.

B.J. Morbitzer – Writer

A person's life is very similar to the annual calendar that records each of the four seasons in chronological order. We see the evidences of the influence of each season across the span of our life.

Chapter 5

Spring
Infancy

"Start children off on the way they should go, and even when they are old they will not turn from it." *(Proverbs 22:6)*

Spring is the season that looks like birth and infancy, covering a period of approximately 15 years of a person's life. It is interesting to note that all the potential that exists in the human personality is already present in the newborn baby.

Jesus spoke a great deal regarding children and this phase of infancy, *"At that time the disciples came to Jesus and asked, 'Who, then, is the greatest in the kingdom of heaven?' He called a little child to him, and placed the child among them. And he said: 'Truly I tell you, unless you change and become like little children, you will never enter the kingdom of heaven. Therefore, whoever takes the lowly position of this child is the greatest in the kingdom of heaven. And whoever welcomes one such child in my name welcomes me.'"* (Matthew 18:1-5)

Spring is a very important season of life since it is the time to be born, grow and prepare for the rest of life. If you have or had children of this age, you know what this phase is like. It is the time for a child to be happy, play, discover things and live without worries. Only parents know how much work children of this age are. It is a time to live free of problems, not having to work or be concerned about paying the bills. If fact, children don't even know where food comes from, they just eat. It is a unique time in life because it is free of worry.

This is the time to be influenced, taught and corrected by parents. Beyond this, it is the season of development and character formation as well as discovery of natural gifts and talents.

King Solomon confirms the importance of this season, *"Start children off on the way they should go, and even when they are old they will not turn from it."* (Proverbs 22:6)

Undoubtedly Spring is the best time for children and adolescents to know God. The earlier the better will be the framework of their growth. It is the most opportune time of their life to transmit the values and principles of the Word of God.

Jesus declared, *"But Jesus called the children to him and said, 'Let the little children come to me, and do not hinder them, for the kingdom of God belongs to such as these. Truly I tell you, anyone who will not receive the kingdom of God like a little child will never enter it.'" (Luke 18:16-17)*

Happy are those who come to know God while they are children, in Spring. How many future problems can be avoided, how many correct decisions can be made because they are well grounded.

Before erecting a building, builders dig down in and place the foundation which is the base for the building. Only after that are the floors above built. The phase of infancy, Spring, is this base.

If you are a young person reading this book, congratulations for your initiative. May reading be one of your good habits. The educator and communicator, Charles T. Jones says the following; **"What you will become will be the result of the books you read, the messages you hear and the friends you have."**

In light of that, continue to read good books, listen to good messages and choose good friends.

Do this in your Spring and God willing, the next seasons will be filled with wisdom, opportunities and blessings!

If you are a parent, take the opportunity to invest in the life of your children. Before you know it they will be grown and leave home. This is the time to influence them and sow good seeds in their lives. What you plant today will be harvested tomorrow. Plant in Spring, because Summer will come soon, with all of its distractions, opportunities and challenges.

Your children need to be well equipped in Spring so they will have the wisdom to survive the high temperatures of Summer.

All of us are going through or have gone through this season and some of us don't even remember it. But one thing is certain; all of us entered the world through it. Even God Himself came into the world going through the seasons He created. Jesus Christ came into the world as a baby and also passed through Spring.

Thank God for Spring! Make the best of it in your life or the life of your children.

Chapter 6

Summer
Youth

"I write to you, young men, because you are strong, and the word of God lives in you, and you have overcome the evil one." (1 John 2:14)

The second season of life is Summer which represents the time of youth. This phase covers approximately the time from 15 to 30 years of age. Summer is the time of heat, strength, expansion and conquest. It is a time of expanding borders, leaving school and going to college and broadening horizons.

The Bible describes youth in the following way:

"The glory of young men is their strength, gray hair the splendor of the old." (Proverbs 20:29)

"I write to you, young men, because you are strong, and the word of God lives in you, and you have overcome the evil one." (1 John 2:14)

Young people need not only physical strength but also spiritual strength.

A little while back I found an old album of photos from when I was a college student. I was 19 years old. I remember that during this time I was part of a musical group from our church that was called "Open Sky".

One day we received an invitation from a church in the city of Perdões, in the south of the state of Minas Gerais. We left Friday night after working all week. We traveled is several cars, carrying with us all our instruments and sound equipment. The trip took all night and we arrived about six in the morning. We rested a bit in the homes of our host families.

In the afternoon we did a program with the youth in the church and we set up our equipment in the movie theater of the city. That evening more than 500 people came to the service and the theater was filled.

The following morning we went to the local jail to bring a word of hope to the prisoners. We then had lunch, loaded all our equipment back in our cars and arrived back in São Paulo at three in the morning. We unloaded everything, slept a little, and at eight we were back to our normal activities. Some went to work and others to the university. It seems crazy. Just remembering this story I get tired.

This is the phase of youth. We have strength, vigor and courage to do many things. Just the same, the young need something more than physical strength, as the Bible teaches,

"Encourage the young men to be self-controlled." (Titus 2:6)

How important it is that young people are prudent and know how to maintain balance between physical strength and wisdom, understanding that there are limits that need to be respected.

For this reason God gives the following counsel to the young, *"In the same way, you who are younger, submit yourselves to your elders. All of you, clothe yourselves with humility toward one another, because, 'God opposes the proud but shows favor to the humble.'" (I Peter 5:5)*

This is the time when young people think they know everything. They think they know more than their parents. Students think they know more than their teachers. Adolescence is a time when the young are becoming adults. Physically they are becoming adults; however, they lack knowledge, experience and wisdom. These are things that come with the passing of the years.

The transformations of this phase are very visible. Hormonal changes happen, whiskers start to grow, the body develops, boy's voices get deeper and the girls start to menstruate. This is why many adolescents have conflicts with their parents; they are living in a different season. This is the clash of seasons. It is the strength and energy of Spring colliding with the wisdom and experience of Summer.

Summer is known for and identified with professional conquests. After college the search for the first job or graduate school comes. This is also a first emotional experiences and challenges. It is distinguished by important decisions, such as courtship, engagement and marriage. A wrong emotional choice in Summer can cause serious difficulties in Fall. However, good choices in Summer guarantee positive results for the rest of life.

If you are in Summer, take care that the intense rays of the sun and the high temperatures do not destroy what was planted in your life in Spring. Tend to the values and principles that were planted by God and your parents.

Stay alert for the plagues and insects that attack the growing plants during Summer. Do not let anyone come and steal the most valuable things you have; your virginity, your dreams, your talents, your abilities, your gifts, your desire to have a family and make a difference in society.

Most certainly this is a time of preparation for a still more promising future. Whatever career you choose - education, business, medicine, engineering, public service or sales, know that in Summer you begin to discover your reason for being. This is the time you begin to work and feel fulfilled with success and your first victories.

The 7 Mountains Strategy

There are "Seven Mountains" of influence that determine and mold the culture in all the nations of the world. They are **Religion** (the Church), **Family**, **Education**, **Government** (Health, Public Safety, Armed Forces), **Media**, **Arts & Sports** and **Business** (Finance, Commerce and Technology). All of us are greatly impacted by these spheres of influence. It is in Summer that we decide to begin engaging one or more of these mountains for the purpose of contributing to the progress of society. For this reason you will need resources, good tools and a good strategic plan.

Summer is the season of opportunities. It is the phase to buy, build, move, move and move.

Priscila and I moved ten times to three different countries in our first ten years of marriage.

You will easily move from city to city, house to house, car to car, job to job or business to business. You will go from one side to the other until you find what you are looking for. It is the time to travel, take risks, run, study, work and take advantage of opportunities. Just the same, this season also has an end. On the calendar the Summer season ends when the first leaves start to Fall.

The Summer of your life ends when the first children start to arrive.

Chapter 7

Fall

Adulthood

"When I was a child, I talked like a child, I thought like a child, I reasoned like a child. When I became a man, I put the ways of childhood behind me." (1 Corinthians 13:11)

Fall is the adult phase and extends approximately from 30 to 60 years of age. It is a time of maturity, experience and wisdom. It is a time to think more carefully and take fewer risks, to be more prudent and less inconsistent.

"When I was a child, I talked like a child, I thought like a child, I reasoned like a child. When I became a man, I put the ways of childhood behind me." (1 Corinthians 13:11)

Unfortunately I know some people who never grew up. They are the size of an adult, the voice of an adult, the body of an adult but they still think as a child or adolescent.

King Solomon shares in the book of Proverbs, a collection of short written sayings. They distill the wisdom and understanding he gained through his life.

He explains that the proverbs are *"for giving prudence to those who are simple, knowledge and discretion to the young." (Proverbs 1:4)*

In other words, the wisdom of these teachings is the fruit of the experience of people who have gone through the season of youth and are in the Fall season of adulthood.

Paul shares this same principle with the older women; *"Then they can urge the younger women to love their husbands and children." (Titus 2:4)*

As we said in the last chapter, Fall begins when children are born and bring great responsibility to the parents. Throughout this season parents will invest time and resources in caring for their children. They will also pass on to them their knowledge and experience.

While children are small, a couple makes many adjustments but as they grow, parents get more quality time for each other.

Fall is a great time to strengthen their relationship, finding creative ways to keep the flame of love burning and to renew their commitment of fidelity.

This is the Psalm of the Fall, adult life.

"Unless the LORD builds the house, the builders labor in vain. Unless the LORD watches over the city, the guards stand watch in vain. In vain you rise early and stay up late, toiling for food to eat— for he grants sleep to those he loves. Children are a heritage from the LORD, offspring a reward from him. Like arrows in the hands of a warrior are children born in one's youth. Blessed is the man whose quiver is full of them. They will not be put to shame when they contend with their opponents in court." (Psalm 127)

Your children are the arrows and you are the warrior. You care for and prepare these arrows so that when Fall comes you can propel them far. You, as a parent, are responsible to propel your children beyond the limitations of your own life.

Cultivate good relationships. This is the time to intensify the bonds with your friends and rejoice in their successes. This is also the time to be child and parent at the same time because you are right in between two generations and two seasons.

In the morning you will take your child to the pediatrician and in the afternoon take your parents to the geriatrician, and if there is still time, you will go see your cardiologist.

In Psalm 127 we also see the importance of working, building, watching, guarding, feeding, having children, warring and even confronting enemies.

It is easy to tell when a person is in Fall. Just as the leaves from the trees change color and Fall, the hair of people starts to get gray and Fall.

Another change happens in the adult body. Metabolism slows down with a corresponding increase in weight. For many this is a constant fight because in this season it is easy to gain weight but loosing it is difficult.

Professionally, it is likely that the career you choose in this stage will continue to the end of your life. For this reason it is extremely important you know what you want to do with your life. That way, at 50 you will not say "I think I chose the wrong path."

In this phase people are more careful and cautious when making decisions. If someone offers some random job or proposes a spectacular deal, the response will certainly be "No, no thanks. This is not for me." Experience and good sense are not taught in college but in the school of life.

Fall also is the time to work to stabilize your professional and financial life. It is necessary to balance economizing in the present with investing in the future Winter that will soon arrive.

Financially, Fall should be the time of great success. What you planted in Spring and cultivated in the Summer will be harvested in Fall.

Fall, without doubt, is the most productive season of your life and certainly these will be the best years of your life.

Chapter 8

Winter

Old age

"Even when I am old and gray, do not forsake me, my God, till I declare your power to the next generation, your mighty acts to all who are to come." (Psalm 71:18)

Winter, best known as old age, is the last season of the year and the last season of life. It begins around 60 and continues until God calls the person home. It is really a great privilege to live all the prior seasons and conclude life in Winter.

Just as Winter is covered with snow, the Winter of life is covered with gray hair.

In *Proverbs 20:29* we read *"The glory of young men is their strength, gray hair the splendor of the old."* Gray hair is a sign of respect, maturity and honor. Even today in many countries, influenced by Great Britain, attorneys and judges use white wigs during trials.

God has a very special promise for His children in Winter. *"They will still bear fruit in old age, they will stay fresh and green." (Psalms 92:14)*

"Even when I am old and gray, do not forsake me, my God, till I declare your power to the next generation, your mighty acts to all who are to come." (Psalm 71:18)

Old age is still a time of fruitfulness, but in a different way because the experience of the previous seasons cannot be ignored. Earlier you worked for the benefit of your children; now, as a senior, you can continue to benefit your children and your grandchildren with your life experience.

Winter brings many challenges; it is the time of vitamin pills and medications.

Whenever I visit my parents I see the containers on the table. It's a medication for this and a vitamin for that. Some are taken with breakfast, others with lunch and others with dinner. But it is still not over.

There are those that need to be taken before going to bed. This is not just the privilege of my parents; it is the ritual of all in this season of life.

Some things cannot be hidden in Winter, for example, wrinkles. They are inevitable. In this phase of life the elderly sleep less and awaken earlier. The tendency is to gain weight and get shorter.

Generally it is during this season, or a bit sooner, the elderly have the great privilege of being promoted to the category of "grandpa and grandma". One wise old grandpa said "Being a grandparent is so great we should have had them before we had children."

This is the time to tell the old stories to your children and grandchildren. Continue to tell your stories, even if your grandchild says he already heard them.

I had the privilege of living with my grandparents in the United States for one year when I was young. I remember my grandparents, Walter and Edelweiss Kaschel, with great fondness. How they helped me. How many times they had me read books aloud and then corrected my pronunciation and helped me understand the material.

My grandfather was a blessing to me. Whenever I had a question about God, the Bible or any other subject, he was always available to sit down with me and answer my questions and concerns in a way that was clear and simple. My grandfather also inspired and taught me to be an interpreter; he was one of the best that ever lived.

Even when my grandparents were in Winter, they had time and patience and love for a grandson that was in the full bloom of Spring.

When you are in this season your greatest satisfaction is to see the success and accomplishments of your children and grandchildren. Your life had significance, had value and was a life well lived.

Now is a time for you to invest in future generations, your children, grandchildren and great-grandchildren. Many call this the phase of "afterglow". Your glow was during the Summer and Fall of your life.

Now that Winter has arrived it is the time for new generations to shine. Therefore, take advantage of every day and every opportunity that God gives you to share your life experiences and leave a legacy for future generations.

As a couple, this is the time to grow old together and fulfill the promises you made before God, "Till death do us part."

Conclusion

Life is short and you can only live it once.

It is impossible to jump over seasons; from Spring to Fall or Summer to Winter.

It is likewise impossible to return to past seasons: from Winter to Fall or Summer to Spring. What is past is past and there is no way to go back.

There is no guarantee that you will finish the season you are in. It could end at any moment. There also is no certainty that you will live to the next season.

The four seasons are an opportunity that God gives you to live and know His marvelous plan for your life.

Winter ends with a sublime experience--when someone takes his last breath and passes from this life. For some this is a moment of fear, doubt and uncertainty and for others it is a moment of joy, peace and victory because they will go and live eternally with their Creator and Savior, Jesus Christ.

The past is a memory, the future is a hope and the present is a gift of God.

Know God through His Son, Jesus Christ and invite Him to enter your life, no matter what season you are in. You will never be the same.

Then, you will understand your reason for living until now and discover the purpose for which you will live from this day forward!

The End...

of the book & the beginning of the rest of your life!

About the author

Mario K. Simoes

♣ International Faculty of Haggai Institute for Advanced Leadership – where he teaches on personal, business and trans-cultural Communications to professionals, businessmen and leaders from emerging nations. He has ministered South Africa, Italy, Singapore, Malaysia, United States, Puerto Rico and Hawaii.

♣ Speaker and Consultant specialized in Leadership, Communications, Motivation and People Management.

♣ Official Interpreter for Gary Chapman (author of the Five Love Languages) John C. Maxwell (#1 Leadership Authority in the United States) in Brazil during speaking engagements to 12.000 people in São Paulo and Brasília in 2008.

♣ Founding President of Preparing Generations International School, bilingual school for children K-12.

♣ Former Public Relations and Communications Advisor for the U.S. Consulate in São Paulo (1995-2001). Personally met President Bill Clinton.

♣ Worked as C.E.O. of the Willow Creek Association, renowned global organization responsible for Leadership Development through the Leadership Summit.

♣ Graduated in Broadcast Journalism from L.S.U. (Louisiana State University), in 1987.

♣ Married to Priscila in 1990 and has 2 sons: Felipe and Davi. Resides in Atibaia, SP – Brazil.

♣ Author of many magazine articles on success, communications, leadership and motivation.

Contact Information

Did you enjoy reading "The 4 Seasons of Life"? Let a family member or a friend know.

Also, write and share with us how this book touched your life. Post your comments about the book on

Facebook: **www.facebook.com/the4seasonsoflife**

To contact Mario K. Simoes, visit the site or send an e-mail.

Site: **www.The4SeasonsofLife.com**

Phones: **(US) 1-919-809-7773**

            (Brazil) 55-11-4411-6333

e-mail: **contact@the4seasonsoflife.com**

Follow Mario Simoes on Twitter:
www.twitter.com/mariosimoes

Other resources, seminars and speaking invitations:

www.mariosimoes.com

www.ingramcontent.com/pod-product-compliance
Lightning Source LLC
Chambersburg PA
CBHW021343090426
42742CB00008B/730